"With American Rice hungry fo
for customers, the joint ventur

MW00876251

KEEP SMILING

AN AMERICAN BUSINESS
IN POST-EMBARGO VIETNAM

Richard McCombs

outskirts
press

Keep Smiling
An American Business in Post-embargo Vietnam
All Rights Reserved.
Copyright © 2021 Richard McCombs
v3.0 r1.0

The opinions expressed in this manuscript are solely the opinions of the author and do not represent the opinions or thoughts of the publisher. The author has represented and warranted full ownership and/or legal right to publish all the materials in this book.

This book may not be reproduced, transmitted, or stored in whole or in part by any means, including graphic, electronic, or mechanical without the express written consent of the publisher except in the case of brief quotations embodied in critical articles and reviews.

Outskirts Press, Inc.
http://www.outskirtspress.com

ISBN: 978-1-9772-3267-0

Cover Photo © 2021 Richard McCombs. All rights reserved - used with permission.

Outskirts Press and the "OP" logo are trademarks belonging to Outskirts Press, Inc.

PRINTED IN THE UNITED STATES OF AMERICA

Dedication

To Claire:

my devoted wife, friend, and companion

Author's Note

In this book, I will use Vietnamese names with diacritics for tones and pronunciation except for Vietnam, Saigon, Hanoi and Mekong Delta. I will also use "Saigon" rather than "Ho Chi Minh City," as almost everyone still refers to the city as "Saigon."

Table of Contents

Foreword

By Ambassador Pete Peterson, first U.S. ambassador to Vietnam after the embargo was lifted.

Keep Smiling is a thoughtful and informative compilation of an American businessman's personal and professional experiences in the early days of Vietnam's open-door economic policy. There are many lessons to be learned about deep-rooted differences in cultural and business practices, and the trials of operating on an often unlevel playing field.

American Rice, one of the first American businesses to enter the newly opened Vietnamese marketplace, had to deal with and overcome the enormous challenges associated with establishing a new business in an emerging market. This candid behind-the-scenes portrayal of how the company worked to overcome the daily perils and obstacles it faced while in Vietnam serves as a contemporary guide for firms contemplating investments in newly emerging economies today.

Many of the author's experiences reminded me of my own challenges as the first postwar American ambassador to

Vietnam, not only in the political and diplomatic spheres but also on the economic front, trying to create a conducive environment for American businesses. Like American Rice, I found no clear-cut road map, unpredictable events, mixed messages, and rudimentary and frequently changing policy, making it difficult to get things done.

The moral of the story is that being first does not always achieve the best outcomes. Over the past 20+ years, Vietnam has grown into a sophisticated economic powerhouse, making a repeat of the American Rice experience highly unlikely.

This book presents a serious business assessment, but it is much more than that. It is an intriguing personal account of an American couple's sudden transition from an American suburbia lifestyle to one in an impoverished, rustic, and developing economy. The story's cast of interesting characters, its historical vignettes, and its sometimes-comical personal sketches make it a fascinating and entertaining read.

Readers will especially appreciate how the authors cleverly weaved into the story a delightful illustration of Vietnamese culture, cuisine, and infrastructure as it was in the early 1990s. Once you pick up *Keep Smiling* you will not put it down until you reach its final page. It will keep you smiling or perhaps even laughing at times!

Foreword

By Prof. Dr. Võ-Tòng Xuân
Rector of Nam Cần Thơ University, Vietnam
Former Vice Rector of the University of Cần Thơ,
Former Rector of An Giang University, and
Former Rector of Tan Tao University

American Rice (ARI) represented the benefits of new technology to Vietnam at the time Vietnam has just re-entered to the international rice export market after 20 years of disruption due to the war. ARI came in to renovate a pre-1975 rice mill taken over by Vinafood, which was like other old mills, equipped with obsolete machineries. However, ARI's new technology meant that ARI was able to pay a premium for high quality rough rice. As Richard mentioned to me in the first year of the American Rice-Vinafood joint venture, ARI obtained much higher milled rice yields and better quality from processing Vietnamese rice than the Vietnamese rice processors due to its significantly better technology.

ARI offered higher prices particularly for higher quality rough rice. Richard consulted with me about encouraging farmers to grow higher quality rice, which I was pleased to do.

I remember sitting in a meeting at the Cần Thơ Communist Party Committee and the Party Secretary stating that Vinafood made a mistake bringing American Rice to Vietnam because ARI was paying higher prices than the Vietnamese rice processors. ARI could pay higher prices because it was able to export rice at $350/MT while the local processors could only export at a price of $200/MT. I remember responding that ARI could pay the higher prices because they had better quality and a trusted brand while the reputation of the Vietnamese processors was extremely poor. We should reward ARI for rendering better profits to our poor farmers. Unfortunately, no one at that time appreciated my comments. Instead they did the contrary, creating a bad precedent, discouraging future cooperation of American businesses.

Ultimately, I believe that ARI was unsuccessful because they were a competitive threat to the local rice processors. The Vietnamese rice industry learned a lot from the ARI participation as brief as it was.

Introduction

After the fall of Saigon in 1975, President Nixon placed a trade embargo on Vietnam that prevented American businesses from investing there. In early 1994, President Clinton ended the embargo.

I oversaw one of the first American companies to return to Vietnam after the embargo was lifted. *Keep Smiling* is about my experiences living and working there while negotiating and operating a joint venture with the government of Vietnam.

I went to Vietnam because I was the only person at American Rice, Inc. (ARI) who volunteered to go. ARI was the largest rice company in the United States.

ARI had been invited to form a joint venture with the largest state-owned rice company in the Socialist Republic of Vietnam. In Vietnam, rice was the most valuable and politically sensitive commodity. ARI's goal was to process rice using ARI's technology and marketing strength and export Vietnamese rice to ARI's global customers. Vietnam's goal was to improve their rice production and expand their exports. Neither entity was clear about how the values and practices of socialism would mix with the business practices of capitalism, but therein lies the story.

There was something about this opportunity that called out to me. To manage the investment, I would have to move to Vietnam, and I wanted my wife to join me. Claire had an active environmental and native land-rights law practice at the time, so she would have to give that up. And we had to rent out the house we'd built a few years earlier and had to pack up our lives to go live in a third world country. Claire had also been an anti-war activist while she was at University of California Berkeley in the 1960s, and she too wanted to see Vietnam. We had hoped that this would be an adventure. Our three children were adults and on their own, so it was just the two of us. The interplay between our personal lives and the challenges I faced in business were a constant for both of us while in Vietnam. It was a risky investment for me, for ARI, and for my wife.

Vietnam's national communist government had almost no experience dealing with capitalism and foreign investors. There was a lot of speculation about how Americans would be received, given Vietnam's recent history. This book explains how this project was perilous, both personally and professionally, and offers an insight into the struggles we had living and working there as well as the struggles Vietnam had with opening the country for business with outsiders. It was exciting. It was an opportunity to be an early pioneer and partner with Vietnam as it opened its doors to the global economy.

For the Vietnamese government, it was a formidable task managing Đổi Mới (the name given to the economic reforms initiated in Vietnam in 1986). Vietnam had been struggling through twenty years of postwar economic challenges, the impacts of the embargo, and disappointments with their political mentors—the Soviet Union and China.

After the American-Vietnamese war, North and South Vietnam became unified and independent of colonial, foreign influences. Vietnam had been fighting invasive and colonial powers for almost 1,000 years, and it had finally realized its dream. As a centrally controlled communist country, the government had begun making all the decisions.

Would the Vietnamese government follow the Chinese development model of state-owned enterprises dominating the country's growth? Would it follow the Korean model of Chaebol or the Hong Kong model in which private companies—with tangible support by the government—become the drivers of change? Or would it follow Singapore's or Taiwan's model? And how would the government choose its path given how important consensus decision-making was in the Vietnamese culture?

Government officials were well-intentioned and open to advice from international bodies such as the United Nations, the World Bank, and the International Finance Corporation (IFC). However, because of their history, they were probably going to be suspicious of foreigners.

By the time ARI was ready to invest in Vietnam, U.S. investors were salivating at the chance to participate in this new market. For twenty years the country had been relatively inaccessible to foreigners—particularly businesses—and there was a sense of expectation in the air. Vietnam had 70 million hardworking, literate, mostly young people living on an average of $1 per day and had only one telephone per ten households. This looked like a landscape in which an optimistic businessperson could create unbelievable opportunities.

THE NOW SOCIETY *Wm. Hamilton*

"It was wild: Same damn helicopters, same damn mad scramble, only this time we're all trying to beat each other into Saigon."
Now Society cartoon. Used with permission of *Newsweek*.
Copyright© 2020. All rights reserved.

I also wondered how I would be received as an American. How would an American rice company be allowed to participate in the most sacred of industries—the rice industry—in Vietnam? Was there enough rice to feed the domestic market and be able to export sufficient rice consistent with our forecast? Was I just naïve, or did I believe that the time was right for new agricultural production technologies—particularly ones which I thought would benefit Vietnam and its people?

While I was not part of the suffering that the American-Vietnamese war caused to both sides (I was a conscientious objector in the war), the war had a dramatic and lasting impact on me, and I wanted to be part of the success of Vietnam's Đổi Mới.

Because ARI was one of the first businesses in post-embargo Vietnam, and because the joint venture was in the critical rice industry, many United States government officials asked to meet with me when they visited Vietnam. Senator Harkin, Senator McCain, and Deputy Secretary Rominger of the USDA all asked to either meet with me in Hanoi or at the JV rice facility in the Mekong Delta. One memorable conversation was in a meeting with Treasury Secretary Robert Rubin. After listening patiently to my complaining about how difficult it was to be one of the first businesses in Vietnam, he said he understood, adding, "You can always tell who the pioneers are because of all the arrows sticking out of their backs."

GOOD MORNING, VIETNAM!

Why would I move to Vietnam to start up and manage one of the first American companies investing in Vietnam after the postwar embargo was lifted? Because the challenge and the opportunity were attractive to me both personally and professionally.

The challenge was particularly perilous, given that the business was rice. Rice is at the heart of Vietnamese and all Southeast Asian cultures and their economies. An investment in this vital industry, so early in the development of Vietnam's post-war economy, was extremely risky. I imagined how we would brand our rice, and the image of a bag of rice with Uncle Sam as American Rice shaking hands with Uncle Ho (Hồ Chí Minh) as the Socialist Republic of Vietnam came to mind.

As I would soon find out, my business skills would need some upgrading. Doing business in postwar Vietnam demanded far more patience and flexibility, and far more smiling, than I ever thought possible. To the casual observer, Vietnam appears to be a land of smiles. When I arrived in 1994, I was struck with the beauty of the land, the constant smiles and laughter, and the graciousness of the people. Even though we were Americans, ARI and I were warmly welcomed. While the smiles always stayed on their faces, I still needed to see what they were really thinking.

And I needed to know, Why me? Was it because I was the chief financial officer (CFO) of both American Rice, Inc. (ARI) and its parent company, ERLY Industries, Inc.? Or was it because I was the only one willing to volunteer to be the general manager of the proposed rice joint venture?

Before what the Vietnamese call "the American War," Vietnam had been a major rice exporter. And ARI believed that Vietnam could renew its position as a major exporter of rice. Plus, the growing world population needed more rice. More than half of the world's population depended on rice as the mainstay of their diet. And yet, at the time, there were only two other major rice-exporting countries—Thailand and the United States. It appeared to be a real opportunity for Vietnam and for ARI.

ARI was the largest rice company in the United States. We had the latest rice-milling technology and many international customers. One of our constraints was not having ample sources of rice to grow our business. ARI could offer its rice-milling technology to Vietnam, while Vietnam could offer to ARI a source of less expensive rice. Together, we could increase our markets and our growth. That was the general idea anyway.

The issues began to emerge early on. While Vietnam offered ARI an opportunity to expand its rice business, the Vietnamese communist government had little experience with foreign capitalism. In 1986, Vietnam initiated some economic reforms known as "Đổi Mới." Before Đổi Mới, in the immediate post-war period, the Vietnamese experienced years of poverty and hunger, especially in the North, where rice production was lower than in the South. For Vietnam, rice was sacred. It was the basis of their cultural, economic, and political survival.

The CEO of American Rice/ERLY Industries, Gerry Murphy, recognized all these risks, and as a successful businessman, he also relished them. Many times, Gerry had proven his ability to manage risks all over the world. Gerry had led ERLY in becoming a global food company by pursuing "a strategy of acquiring troubled agribusiness enterprises with strong upside potential."[1]

As the CFO, I wanted to contain the risk. So I recommended that we limit our investment in Vietnam to $1 million. However, with such a small budget, none of the production managers at ARI were willing to move to Vietnam and take responsibility for starting a joint venture there. Maybe they just did not want to leave their comfortable homes in the U.S. to move to a third world country on such an uncertain mission.

After asking for volunteers and receiving none, Gerry turned to me and suggested that since I'd set the financial limitation on the investment, I should be willing to move to Vietnam to manage the joint venture. He made it sound like I'd already agreed to go.

He also knew that I was never afraid to take on a challenge—especially when no one else would dare touch it. So I said I'd consider it. But asking my wife, Claire, to come with me was another matter entirely.

Claire and I were both engaged in anti-war activities in the 1960's and '70s. Our activities were based on both a love of peace and our sense that the war had ravaged Vietnam and had sacrificed American lives. It was because of our historical connection to Vietnam that we considered taking this on.

We agreed to go see the country to help us decide if we could live there. We went about getting our passports and visas in order and prepared for our first visit. The next few months for me were a heady mix of expectations about what I might accomplish with this extraordinary challenge. I was also concerned about the practical realities of living and working in a completely different world. Our mild Northern California Mediterranean climate would turn into the hot and humid tropics. Our quiet, relatively easy life in the suburbs would turn into the busy, noisy urban world with an unknown language and culture and the constant pressure to, basically, not mess up. And all my business experiences would be challenged on every level.

I consulted some friends who knew Vietnam, either as their homeland or from being there during the war. I understood from them that keeping my cool was key. One advisor said, "Never let them make you upset or show them anger." Another said to respect their graciousness and learn their manners but not to be fooled by them. I decided that smiling would be my personal passport. Keeping a straight face comes naturally to me, but my smile turned out to be essential. Smiling carried me through the next four tumultuous years.

Imagine these scenes:

- Early on, I was sitting in Vinafood II's conference room in their offices in Saigon. Vinafood II, a state-owned enterprise, was about to become our joint venture partner. Because I was used to a much faster paced and focused meeting style, I found this meeting to be extremely boring. I was to learn that this was often the case. Was it because the translations from English to Vietnamese took so long? English is a straightforward language compared to the subtle intonations and complex meanings of words in Vietnamese. Was it that the endless cups of green tea were getting to me? Was it because the process of getting the agreement with a joint venture partner was getting tedious? Or was it because the wooden seat on which I sat was so hard? I decided to Keep Smiling so that everyone else in the room would be willing to continue.
- Later, I was sitting in the office of the State Committee for Cooperation Investments (SCCI) in Hanoi. The translators were talking (arguing?) in Vietnamese about the clauses in the proposed joint venture license. I had spent five months negotiating a joint venture contract and now I felt as if I were starting all over again with the Vietnamese government. Keep Smiling.
- I remember sitting in my office with the representative of the Communist Party employed by the ARI-Vinafood Joint Venture. Having a Party representative is a position that is required by all companies. He was lecturing me at length on why he needed to have the 250 salaried employees of the joint venture take all of Thursday

afternoons each week to attend communist education classes. Keep Smiling.

- During the shipment of rice to Iran, I sat across from Iranian rice inspectors, who were tasked with the inspection of *every* bag of rice being shipped to Iran under our 160,000-metric-ton contract. The inspectors were upset because we had already started loading the first ship before they had arrived. The problem was that since the first shipment would consist of over 300,000 bags of rice, it was obvious that the inspection was going to go very slowly. The ship was not going to stay docked there interminably without the joint venture paying huge demurrage payments. Keep Smiling.

- I was sitting in my office with the chief inspector of the widely feared Government Inspectorate, the equivalent of the state-security police. He was telling me about what he characterized as the "serious charges" against ARI and why we were being investigated. The chief inspector listed all the Communist Party principles in his explanation about why the investigation was serious, and he was hell-bent on me taking him seriously. Apparently, it was not a part of the Vietnamese government's original plan that we capitalists would be successful in their socialist republic. Keep Smiling.

How could I have possibly appreciated at that time what would be involved in (1) moving to Vietnam, (2) starting a joint venture with a large Vietnamese state-owned company, and (3) managing a company with entirely Vietnamese staff while not understanding their language and culture? Naivety did not even begin to describe my grasp of the situation.

But fortune smiled on me—at least at the beginning. One of our employees at American Rice, Inc., Bill Bond, was married to Mai Shinn, an American-Vietnamese woman, who was a nurse and mother of two young children. They were willing to move to Vietnam, and Bill was willing to take on managing the production aspects of the project.

Then another fortunate turn came when I advertised for an accountant who spoke Vietnamese. When Kevin "Kiệt" Nguyễn showed up for his interview in the Fairmont Hotel lobby in San Francisco, I could tell he was the right person, and I hired him almost immediately. Kiệt had grown up in Vietnam, had moved to the U.S. after the war, had earned an accounting degree, and was excited about returning to his native country. And of course, Kiệt would have a much better understanding of the culture than I ever could.

Kiệt was a Việt Kiều, which literally means "Overseas Vietnamese" and refers to Vietnamese people living outside of Vietnam. By far the largest community of Việt Kiều live in the United States. Of the 4.5 million Overseas Vietnamese, a majority left Vietnam as economic and political refugees after the 1975 overthrow of Saigon and the North Vietnamese takeover of the pro-U.S. South Vietnam.

Once I had my two in-country team members, I was ready to deal with the 250 salaried employees and the 500–1,000 manual laborers who were already working at the rice facility. One thing was clear, I would need to Keep Smiling to have any chance of success in Vietnam.

2

American Rice: Why Vietnam?

Gerry Murphy hired me in 1990 as CFO of ERLY Industries, Inc. (ERLY), a publicly held food company with subsidiaries in juice, rice, wine, a forest fire retardant business, and an international agricultural consulting firm. Before joining ERLY, I was CEO of Italian Swiss Colony Wines (ISC Wines), which was the second largest winery in California with five separate wineries. I also had planted a vineyard in Sonoma County, so I knew something about wine, but nothing about rice. One of ERLY's largest subsidiaries was Comet Rice. Since I needed to learn about the products sold by Comet Rice, I moved to Comet Rice's headquarters in Houston, Texas, and began my crash course in the rice industry.

Comet Rice owned 48% of another rice company, American Rice, Inc. (ARI), which was also based in Houston. It was clear to Gerry that if we could combine the two rice companies, ERLY would achieve substantial efficiencies in processing and marketing rice. The resulting company would be the largest rice company in the U.S., with facilities in Texas, Arkansas, Louisiana, and California.

Gerry approached the CEO of ARI, John Howland, about joining the two companies, and Mr. Howland agreed. As was typical
of Gerry's deals, the transaction immediately became complicated, not that this would stop him. A history of American Rice,
Inc. noted that "the proposed merger involved two steps. First,
ERLY's Comet Rice subsidiary would transfer its 48% interest in
ARI back to ERLY Industries. Second, ARI would acquire Comet
from ERLY for 17.2 million shares of ARI stock. The result was
that ERLY controlled more than 75% of ARI. The transaction was
delayed for two years while ERLY struggled to secure adequate
financing. The merger was eventually concluded in June 1993."[2]

I remember this transaction very well since by then I was both
the CFO of ERLY and acting CFO of ARI. It was my responsibility to obtain the necessary financing. That meant I had many
sleepless nights in Texas during those two years. (I had been
through this before during my time as CEO of ISC Wines.)
But we completed the financing. After the merger of ARI and
Comet Rice, ERLY's rice business was once again ready to grow
rapidly and to seek new opportunities.

The combined companies were called American Rice, Inc.

The two companies were purchasing over 40% of the U.S.
rough-rice crop. ARI would not be able to grow without new
sources of rough (or paddy) rice. In addition, the two companies' facilities were operating at close to capacity, so processing
capacity was also limited. We began to look for new sources of
rough rice outside the United States.

One of ERLY's employees was Urbain Tran. Urbain had been
born in Vietnam, and his father had been an active participant

in the Vietnamese rice industry. After seeing the results of the Tet Offensive by the North Vietnamese Army in 1968, Urbain's family had moved to the U.S. Urbain spoke English, Vietnamese, and Chinese. He was one of the most personable men I have ever met, and we became close friends. It was through Urbain that a joint venture in Vietnam began to take shape.

After the ARI/Comet merger, Gerry asked Urbain where we could source more rice internationally and how we could expand our rice business. At the time, Thailand was a major world exporter, but Urbain knew that the Thai rice industry, and particularly the Thai rice export industry, was fully developed, and thus there was no room for an outsider to set up business there. Also, Urbain knew that Vietnam had historically been an exporter of rice, but its industry was only beginning to recover after the American-Vietnamese war ended. The postwar trade embargo had prevented American companies from doing any business with Vietnam. There were no other countries in the world that consistently produced and exported rice.

Both Gerry and Urbain were optimistic that the U.S. trade embargo would be lifted. Urbain persuaded Gerry to let him research the possible opportunities for ARI in Vietnam. As soon as Vietnam began encouraging foreign investment, Vietnam's prime minister, Võ Văn Kiệt, invited 100 international businesspeople to learn about doing business in Vietnam.

Urbain was invited to attend, and it would be his first return trip to Vietnam since he and his family had left in 1968. When he got there, he told the prime minister that he was only interested in the rice industry. At a reception for the invited guests, the minister of agriculture, Nguyễn Công Tạn, came up to Urbain and said, "You must be the rice guy." After that, Urbain and Minister Tạn (who also spoke Chinese after his studies in China) became trusted friends.

Urbain's research outlined how ARI could invest in Vietnam. It was clear that the Vietnamese government would be cautious about foreign investment and, as China had done initially, Vietnam would require all foreign investment to be done through joint ventures with Vietnamese state-owned companies. Urbain's effort was to identify which Vietnamese companies would make the best partners.

The Vietnamese rice export industry was controlled by two government-owned companies, Vinafood I and Vinafood II. The former was based in North Vietnam, the latter in the South. Having grown up in Saigon, Urbain was most familiar with the Southern Vietnamese rice industry. And South Vietnam had the largest rice crops, so it was a straightforward choice to consider working with Vinafood II.

Also, Vinafood II (VF) had a large rice-processing facility in Trà Nóc, a town in the Mekong Delta.

VF escorted Urbain around South Vietnam and showed him VF's rice facility in Trà Nóc. Urbain quickly realized that the Trà Nóc facility needed all of the improvements that ARI had to offer, including ARI's newest rice-sorting technology. It also needed a good cleaning.

Urbain was very thoughtful about how he marketed ARI's entry into Vietnam. For example, he emphasized that ARI was in the Vietnamese market "for the long term." This was unlike some of the other international companies who were just out to grab an emerging market. Urbain was also instrumental in the initial plans for how ARI could form the joint venture (JV) with VF and had numerous meetings with VF's general manager, Madame Dương Thị Ngọc Triều. Once the JV was formed and operational, he was a key advisor to both the ARI team as they interfaced with VF as well as Minister Tạn.

Gerry Murphy, VF Director Muoi Tạn, me, and Urbain Tran

ARI had a worldwide reputation for selling high quality rice, and now its primary objective was to acquire a source of exportable rice to meet the demands of its international customers.

Vietnam's reputation in the international market was as a producer of low-quality and thus low-priced rice. ARI could bring its rice-processing technology to Vietnam, which would improve the quality of Vietnamese rice. ARI would then sell Vietnam's rice to ARI's international customers at a cheaper price than ARI's U.S. rice. In addition, the JV could import Vietnamese rice to the U.S., blend it with ARI's U.S. rice, and lower the cost to ARI for the U.S. domestic market.

The Vietnamese government wanted us to invest in Vietnam to upgrade their technology, improve rice quality thus obtaining higher prices, increase its exports, and improve its balance of payments.

After the joint venture was established, Gerry took a personal interest in the project and made frequent trips to Vietnam. Gerry enjoyed visiting the Trà Nóc facility to observe the operations but never interfered unlike how many international company CEOs managed their subsidiaries.

Gerry observing the purchasing and drying of rough rice

To accomplish all ARI's objectives, ARI's plan was to become one of the largest rice processors and exporters in Vietnam by exporting over 200,000 metric tons (MT) of rice per year to our existing and new customers.

3

The Saigon River Jazz Band

Landing at Tân Sơn Nhất International Airport in Saigon for the first time was memorable. Of course, Claire and I were excited, but also exhausted from the long flight from San Francisco with a stop in Hong Kong. Although Saigon had been renamed Hồ Chí Minh City after the war, we found that everyone still called it Saigon, so we did too. And we felt that by saying "Saigon," the word somehow brought together the reality of where we were and evoked the deep feelings that we had about the possibility of moving there and being part of Vietnam's recovery from the American-Vietnamese war.

As the plane began its descent over the South China Sea, I looked out the window to catch our first glimpse of Vietnam. I saw an intensely green and watery world of rice paddies. Then the land changed into a mass of grey concrete third world urban sprawl wrapped around the snaking curves of a wide river. Saigon spread out as far as the eye could see.

Just before we landed, the large Quonset huts built for the war came into view. It reminded us of the images we saw, less than twenty years before, of Americans and Vietnamese families who scrambled to leave the country from this same airport.

Like most Americans, I had experienced the American-Vietnamese war from black-and-white television and newspaper reports. Arriving in Vietnam brought back strong memories of those images. When I saw large round depressions in the ground that were full of water, I originally thought that they were irrigation or fishponds. I later found out they were bomb craters. But, as with everything in Vietnam at the time, they were repurposed for the country's economic development.

Then, after landing, as the plane began to taxi along the tarmac, the reality of life in Vietnam in 1994 presented itself. An old green station wagon with a flashing light on the roof pulled up in front of the plane. It had a large sign in English on top that read, "FOLLOW ME." Then it drove slowly along in front of the plane, guiding us to the terminal, looking like a tiny turtle dragging a huge silver ship behind it all the way.

There were no Jetways. We climbed down the portable steel steps and were immediately hit with the full-body impact of incredible heat and humidity. We walked over to the terminal, up several flights of steps, and stood in line for a long time, sweating, and hoping that our paperwork was in order. The young, new immigration officers took forever with each passenger, asking questions and reading documents repeatedly. The officer made sure we declared that everything we brought into Vietnam would be taken back out with us when we left. This was our first of what was to become a daily practice of adjusting our expectations as Americans to the reality of living in Vietnam. It was always going to be slow, uncertain, and extremely hot.

Urbain met us at the airport and drove us through what looked like total chaos in the streets to our hotel. He wanted to reassure us that the poverty we saw was a fact of life in Vietnam, almost as if he wanted to soften our culture shock. But what we saw was an incredibly complex life speeding past us, not slums.

We also noticed how insane the traffic was. There were no distinct traffic lanes, and what few traffic lights that did exist went green and red without any impact on the drivers. The streets were filled with bicycles, cyclos, motorcycles, pedestrians, trucks, busses, and only a few cars. And sometimes crates of chickens. There seemed to be an air of "anything goes."

The noises were deafening. Anyone who had a horn was constantly using it, rather than brakes, to get through the mass of moving objects. Motorcycles zipped by with three and four persons, sometimes with whole families, on each motorcycle. And yet somehow, like all Vietnam, the traffic worked, noisily, chaotically. And while it was fascinating to watch, it was not something we wanted to try driving in ourselves.

When we arrived at our hotel, the Saigon Omni, we were delighted to see how beautiful and comfortable the new hotel was. The Omni was one of the few recently constructed modern hotels in Saigon, perhaps in the entire country. And although it was not centrally located, it soon became our home base.

Most of the international hotels in the downtown area were still stuck in the 1960s in terms of décor and attitude. They had hard, wooden single beds with silky flowered bedspreads, and a single washbasin in each room. The bathrooms, then standard in Vietnam, were a combination shower/toilet. So you had to get the sequence right, or the toilet was all wet.

While these hotels were great for tourists who were coming back to relive life there during the war, they were not a place where we could stay at length and be functional in business. We did not have an office yet. Cell phones were just being introduced, and that helped. But we were still under the illusion that we could be basically functional in a few weeks. That soon dissolved.

On the first few days of our first trip, we found that just sending a fax was a major undertaking. Fortunately, they had enough English-speaking censors to read our correspondence as it was sent outside Vietnam. But we heard that the Swedish visitors had to wait three or four days for their faxes to go through. Evidently very few Vietnamese spoke Swedish.

While we were on our exploratory first trip, Vinafood (as a state-owned enterprise, not exactly independent of the government) suggested Claire and I live in Saigon. We later came to understand that these "suggestions" were nicely put orders and not real choices. Since we wanted to please our hosts, we spent days looking at potential places to live. They showed us houses that they owned and hoped that we would rent from them. One was a crumbling classic French colonial compound on Điện Biên Phủ Street (prior to 1975 it was called Phan Thành Gian Street) for which they expected a typical monthly rent of over $13,000![3] The house had separate quarters for the cooks, cleaners, and gardeners. It was in dismal condition. Later I realized that Vinafood wanted to rent it to us so that we would upgrade it for them.

I was constantly catching up to even the most basic appreciation of what life was going to be like in a centrally planned economy. My insights came constantly while living in Vietnam, but mostly they came to me well after the fact. So much of what I know now is understood in hindsight. It took me a long time to gain even the most superficial understanding of the country and especially what it meant to be doing business there, an effort that continued throughout my entire experience in Vietnam.

After an exhausting search, it did not look possible to live in Saigon. Claire loved the architecture but did not want to live like a French colonist. Nor did we intend to take over these beautiful but crumbling mansions and turn them into showcases. Some foreign investors were doing that, particularly the large Asian ones, and they did a beautiful job. But it was far too expensive to consider. Then it was "suggested" that we could live in a gated area of new homes that was in a suburb outside the city. This was a walled community of stucco and tile-roofed homes: a new development built and reserved for expats. It was clearly a country-club life. And neither Claire nor I were interested in that lifestyle.

We wanted to live more modestly and alongside the Vietnamese. Why else would we undertake this challenge if not to experience life in Vietnam, not some cookie-cutter expat life set apart from the host country? I began to wonder if it was even going to be possible to live in Vietnam. The daily onslaught of noise, crowds, and heat, and the constant challenges of learning another culture and customs, were both exhilarating and stressful. I was not there as a tourist. I felt a strong obligation to be a good contributor. I wanted to learn how to best engage with the Vietnamese as business partners and to have a personal life that functioned as well.

When Urbain realized that Claire and I were not finding somewhere to be comfortable living in Vietnam, he decided we needed to see how others there lived. He took us to visit a friend of his, Nguyễn Tuyet Mai and her Thai partner, Sid, who lived on the outskirts of Saigon.

We drove there in a taxi, weaving our way out of town and then down a long dirt road lined with palms further into the green jungle along the winding Saigon River. Suddenly we came upon a place that was stunningly beautiful. And quiet. The home was exquisitely done in Balinese style, all open air with silk curtains moving in the slight breeze coming off the river.

Our hosts were gracious and welcoming. It was Sunday afternoon, the day of the week that they always held a party with live music. Mai was a jazz singer, and she had her own group: the Saigon River Jazz Band.

They played great old jazz and blues standards in an open pavilion on the lawn just below the house. It was lined with couches and cushions for lounging. We were charmed and entranced. And then we were fed the best Vietnamese food we had ever eaten.

This was the relaxation we had craved: cool breezes off the river and cool jazz wafting around us. Thanks to Urbain's astute intuition, we ended the day thinking maybe we could find a way to live in Vietnam after all.

Saigon River Jazz Band playing at Mai's house

Our next stop was to visit the rice factory VF owned in Trà Nóc, in the heart of the Mekong Delta. The trip took five hours, driving along raised levy roads clogged with traffic in a van that did not have shocks but clearly had a loud horn. In the van with Claire and I were Madame Triều and several of her people. The roads were full of chaotic traffic and lined with stands selling housewares, foods, and hundreds of people selling small items to every passerby as well as a few who were begging for handouts.

We had to cross two tributaries of the Mekong River on ferries. As the lines of cars and vans waited to load onto the ferries and on the ferries themselves, the vendors were calling out to sell their goods. Others pressed their faces to the windows of the van to look inside. They might have wondered why these Americans were back in the Mekong Delta.

The Trà Nóc rice-processing facility was located on the Sông Hậu River, a tributary of the Mekong River, and was located near the third largest city in Vietnam, Cần Thơ. Being located on the river meant that rough (paddy) rice could be delivered directly to the facility by the local farmers, then dried and milled, and finally the finished rice could be loaded and transported to the port for shipping.

The facility was larger than I had expected. It covered over 17 hectares (about 40 acres) and consisted of five separate rice mills, a large office building, and a two-story canteen that prepared and served food to the workers. It needed upgrading.

Trà Nóc rice-processing facility

It was attractive to ARI since VF was willing to include the rice facility in the joint venture as their capital contribution. One significant benefit to ARI was that rice processing could begin much more quickly since the facility was already built.

From a personal point of view, it quickly became attractive to live and work alongside such an impressive river, really one of the world's wonders.

The Mekong River originates in Tibet and flows through China, Laos, Thailand, and Cambodia before it reaches Vietnam. Once there, it forms a massive delta. The name of the Mekong in Vietnamese is Song Cu'u Long, or Nine-tailed Dragon River. The Vietnamese know that there are only eight tributaries, but because nine is a lucky number, it is known as the "nine-tailed dragon." And there are plenty of streams that can be counted as the ninth tail, as all the rivers of the Mekong fan out and drain into the East Vietnam Sea.

The river traffic was a constant parade of large and small boats. Whole families lived on the large crafts. The bows of the old wooden working boats were painted with bright red surrounding a pair of eyes to "watch for traffic" and with a painted anchor for a "nose."

It was not the provincial town or the rice mill that attracted us. It was the magic of this magnificent river.

Unlike the urban life in Saigon, Trà Nóc and even the Cần Thơ area felt more manageable and more welcoming to us. I loved the river, and since I knew most of my time would be spent at the rice facility, I decided to see if we could move to the Mekong Delta.

However, the housing options in Cần Thơ were grim or non-existent. Still, we persisted. Then, while exploring the Trà Nóc facility (it was so large that it was more like a small town), we found a concrete building near the canteen. It had a small yard out front and several rooms.

We thought maybe we could make that work. There were no toilets though, just an open trench in the back of the building. The senior staff parked their motorcycles inside because it was so convenient. And the fact that there was no bedroom, no bathroom, and no kitchen? And no furnishings? Well, we were up for a challenge.

By the time we arrived in the Mekong Delta, the Vietnamese who'd fought for or worked with the U.S. in the American-Vietnamese war were mostly gone. No other Americans lived there, and hardly anyone spoke English. Occasionally, a local would come up and ask if I was Russian. Older ones approached me speaking French. When they found out I was an American, a few came forward to tell us about what they had done for the Americans during the war.

4

This Is Beginning to Get Serious

After Urbain had discussed the outline of an agreement with Vinafood II in 1993, I thought that the negotiations would proceed smoothly. The embargo had not yet been lifted, but we were confident that the new venture was possible. I quickly learned that many difficult negotiations were just about to begin.

Urbain had recommended VF as the ideal partner since they were the largest rice processor and exporter in Vietnam. They were a state-owned company, and they seemed quite open to working with us. Their general manager was Madame Dương Thị Ngọc Triều.

Madame Triều was very well connected to the Vietnamese government. We were hoping that meant she could make sure that the JV would receive their support. Her father had lived in the jungle in South Vietnam during the American-Vietnamese war (during the war, there were two communist governments—one in the North and one in the South). He was Minister of Economy for the Provisional Revolutionary

Government (PRG) of the Republic of South Vietnam until re-unification with the North was completed. He continued in that role once reunification occurred.

Madame Triều and her siblings had been sent to Hanoi as young teenagers to learn about the communist government. Hồ Chí Minh called them the "Southern School Pupils." After reunification and having been trained in the North, they were given important responsibilities, such as in the rubber and oil industries, imports, and exports from the South, and of course, the rice industry. Madame Triều was placed in the rice industry. Triều's father was a friend of Prime Minister Võ Văn Kiệt. Her father and the prime minister lived in the jungle together during the war. Madame Triều maintained the relationship with the prime minister.

Claire and Madame Triều

On my first visit to Vietnam in early 1994, Claire and I met Madame Triều in Cần Thơ as we prepared to visit the Trà Nóc rice-processing facility. She was very charming.

For such a powerful woman, I was impressed by how frugal Madame Triều was. She led a modest life. When she visited the Trà Nóc rice facility, she stayed in a room with no bathroom or privacy. When I mentioned this to her, she said that during the war, she had lived with her siblings in the jungle, living on a diet of salt and rice.

My initial meetings with Madame Triều were very pleasant. She clearly wanted the JV to go forward. I remember her giving me "motherly advice" to consult with Trà Nóc's existing managers, the Communist Party representative, and the Labor representative. She even told me that if I were a success, then I might even want to join the Party. However, once we began negotiating the terms of the JV, the relationship became more strained.

I was sure that Madame Triều would recognize the benefits of associating with such a reputable company as American Rice. ARI had a team of knowledgeable employees who could help me bring ARI's technology to Vietnam.

ARI knew going into the project that we would only be allowed to export rice and not be able to sell rice in the domestic market. Consequently, we were determined to be able to export enough rice to ensure the viability of the JV. We also knew that rice was the most important food for the Vietnamese people, and the rice industry was practically a religion in Vietnam. A large percentage of the Vietnamese population, almost 70%

at the time, worked in the rice industry. But we also knew that after the American-Vietnamese war, the country had experienced massive food shortages.

After visiting the Trà Nóc facility, Urbain and I intended to complete the negotiations for the Joint Venture Agreement. It proceeded very slowly, probably because once VF believed that ARI was committed to the JV, they began the "slow dribble." This was a predictable negotiating tactic intended to obtain the best terms for them. Their position was that they had all the time in the world.

After numerous meetings, I wrote to Claire. I said, well, "I am still here and alive but not quite sure for how long. Trying to get things done here is a challenge. Until we have the JV Agreement signed, there is little getting done since no one will make decisions except Madame Triều."

Madame Triều was also watching which way the wind was blowing in Hanoi. In one meeting, I remember sitting on a hard, wooden chair for eight hours as we tried to reach an agreement on issues to which I thought we had already agreed. Madame Triều was an excellent negotiator. Every time we'd made a further commitment to being in Vietnam, she knew she could extract more concessions. It was days and days of delays and delays.

At one point, I was waiting for VF staff to review the changes I'd proposed earlier in the week. They knew I was scheduled to leave Wednesday. I was counting on getting the agreement signed on Tuesday. I naively assumed that it would be signed late Tuesday night, as there were no new issues. Instead, I learned that I could never assume anything.

I came to expect this strategy: they would wait until they knew I was leaving to finalize things. It was used so frequently that I began to tell them I was leaving a day before I was ticketed to leave. That way I could refuse the new conditions they tried to include and tell them that I would just "delay my flight."

By the end of July, I still did not have a signed agreement. I was ready to give up. I decided it was time to pack up and go home. There was nothing more to gain by sticking around. We would negotiate something, agree on it, and then the next day, they would act like they'd never agreed. I came to understand that there was absolutely no benefit to trying to make compromises just to make a deal.

On one occasion, I think they assumed that I would have to make another trip to Saigon to finalize the agreement. I'd prepared all the documents, had the final changes done on the hotel's word processor, printed it out, and signed all of them. I told them that I wasn't staying any longer—take it or leave it. I also put a "zinger" in the document, which they could see very quickly. My goal was to waste time negotiating the zinger to minimize the time spent negotiating any new economic issues. We spent hours arguing about the zinger, and I began to feel confident that I had developed a successful strategy for the JV negotiations.

But I must give Madame Triều credit. When we got down to the last $100,000 difference in positions, she said she didn't have any more time (and I thought I was the one who had to catch a plane!) and that she was sorry, but if we wanted an agreement, we had to agree to her final offer. She said that she could leave her people to sign the document. Otherwise she was sorry that we had spent so long on this and didn't have a deal. Brilliant strategy. Keep Smiling.

On my flight home, I realized that the Vietnamese didn't have the same attitude about time as I did. We burned up the dollars by camping out in Saigon. They didn't really have a personal stake in this transaction and probably had some risk of being criticized, regardless of the terms of the agreement. They needed to play out these negotiating sessions for all they were worth. I had no choice, and I accepted their position and signed the agreement.

Having completed the Joint Venture Agreement with a prominent state-owned company, I then assumed that the government approval would be straightforward. Little did I realize that the *real* negotiations would happen when we went to the State Committee for Cooperation and Investments (SCCI) to obtain our JV license.

The Vinafood team and me outside the SCCI offices

One of the more amusing issues was providing the SCCI with the financial statements of both American Rice and Vinafood. The picture below shows me holding the VF financial statements in two boxes weighing about five pounds in my right hand and the 8.5"x11" ARI annual report in my left hand.

VF financials in the boxes and ARI financials in my left hand

When the JV license was finally granted on October 15, 1994, both parties were committed to $17.9 million of Total Investment Capital and $5.4 million of Legal Capital, the latter being the only real commitment. ARI had agreed to provide $3 million of the Legal Capital for 55% ownership of the JV. VF had agreed to provide the land use rights and the Trà Nóc facility, which were valued at $2.4 million. It was a twenty-year agreement with the principal activities being the "processing and marketing of white and parboil rice."

ANNOUNCEMENT

AMERICAN RICE - VINAFOOD CO., LTD.

A Joint Venture Company established between:

AMERICAN RICE, INC.
and
CENTRAL FOOD CORPORATION II (VINAFOOD II)

*Has been issued by SCCI investment
license No. 1011/GP dated 15 October*

Total Investment Capital:	US$ 17,930,000
Legal Capital:	US$ 5,380,000
Foreign Party:	ARI 55%
Vietnamese:	Vinafood 45%
Duration:	20 years
Principal Activities:	Processing and marketing white and parboil rice

BOARD OF MANAGEMENT

Chairman:	Mr. Gerald D. Murphy (American)
Vice Chairman:	Mrs. Duong Thi Ngoc Trieu (Vietnamese)
Members:	Mr. Douglas Murphy (American)
	Mr. Richard McCombs (American)
	Mr. Phan Van Tan (Vietnamese)
General Director:	Mr. Richard McCombs (American)
Deputy General Director:	Mr. Phan Van Tan (Vietnamese)
Head Office:	Tra Noc Rice Mill
	Can Tho Province, Vietnam
	Tel: (84) 71 41299 - Fax: (84) 71 141203

When we finally received the license, we celebrated with an elaborate and expensive dinner at a restaurant in Hanoi. ARI was expected to pay, of course. And all the principles were there, including Mr. Nghĩa, who was Deputy Director of VF. I found out later that the restaurant was owned by Mr. Nghĩa. Keep Smiling.

Next, ARI asked for the newly licensed JV to have a board meeting. On November 3, 1994, I was unanimously voted to be the first general director. And only then did I realized that, indeed, this was beginning to get serious.

5

Global Rice and
Vietnamese Rice

Rice is perhaps the most important cereal crop in the world. It has been cultivated by humans for about 8,000 years, having originated in the great river deltas of Southeast Asia, although some varieties were also grown in Africa and India. It is important nutritionally, culturally, economically, and politically.

At a 1994 conference in Hanoi, Klaus Lampe, Director General of the International Rice Research Institute (IRRI), summarized the global rice industry at the time.

- Each year, the world's population increases by almost 100 million people and population growth is not expected to level off until the middle of the 21st century at the earliest. Feeding these 100 million more people every year is the biggest challenge of the next decades.
- Rice is the basic staple food for half the world.
- More than 90% of the world's rice is grown and consumed in Asia, home to more than 50% of the world's poor and more than 90% of the world's rice farmers.
- Only 4% of rice production is traded on the world market.[4]

As American Rice was negotiating the Joint Venture Agreement in Vietnam, the U.S. Department of Agriculture in their October 1994 *Rice Situation Report* projected world rice production (milled basis) to be about 352.1 million metric tons (MT). Due to increasing world consumption, ending inventories would decline to 44.4 million MT, the lowest since 1982/83. This decline was almost entirely due to the decline in inventories in China.

Thailand maintained its position as the world's largest exporter in 1995, exporting 4.5 million MT, representing over 30% of its production. The United States, the second largest exporter, was expected to export 2.7 million MT or about 40% of its production.

The third largest exporter, Vietnam, had its second largest crop on record, 14.9 million MT, and was expected to export 2.1 million MT, which was only 14% of its production. These exports were up from almost zero exports in 1989.

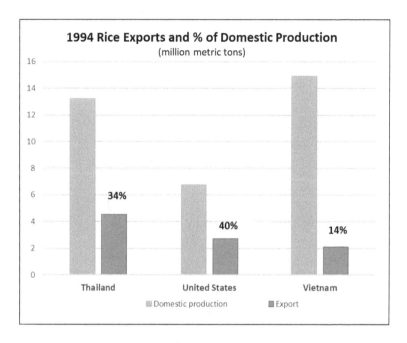

1994 Rice Exports and % of Domestic Production
(million metric tons)

Source: USDA October 1994 Rice Situation Report

For Vietnam, a small change in exports as a percent of production meant that Vietnamese exports might fluctuate significantly. With only two other countries exporting significant portions of their rice production, rice companies in the United States had limited reliable quantities of rice outside the U.S.

Among the three exporters, export prices for Vietnamese rice were the lowest because the quality was significantly lower. One of the reasons for the lower quality was the larger percent of "brokens." Brokens occurred during drying and milling. Vietnamese technology was minimal to avoid the cause of brokens and to sort out brokens once they occurred. As an example, solar drying of rough rice in Vietnam often occurred alongside the roads, and passing vehicles driving over the rough rice caused broken rice.

Pricing differences reflected this quality difference. In 1994, U.S. prices for high-quality rice were $375/MT, Thai high-quality rice sold for $260/MT, and Vietnamese high-quality rice only sold for $216/MT.[5]

Vietnam's rice industry is a mirror of its culture and social fabric. Rice to the Vietnamese is both sacred and life supporting. One example is illustrated in "The Miraculous Plant" as described in *Vietnamese Folk-Tales*:[6]

A tramp arrived at a village, completely worn out. He had eaten nothing for two days. Hunger gave him a bright idea.

He went whispering into people's ears: "I know a miraculous plant, which can revive even a man at the edge of the grave. I am willing to share my secret."

A rich man hastened to invite him to his house and treated him to a sumptuous meal.

When all was over, the host tactfully recalled the promise about the wonder plant.

"Come along with me," said the guest. "It's in the neighborhood."

They went out together, with all the secrecy required.

When he found himself at a good distance from the village, the rogue stopped and pointed his finger at a rice field.

"Here grows the miraculous plant," he said.

"What? Rice? You're not joking?"

"Certainly not! Without the rice I've just eaten at your home, I'd be dead at this hour!"

And the rascal took to his heels.

The International Rice Research Institute (IRRI) studied and developed new rice varieties, and one variety was highly desired in Vietnam. IRRI had introduced a new rice variety called IR8 and farmers' yields began steadily improving. Vietnamese farmers once again had a chance to prosper and maybe even afford a Honda motorcycle. Those who did called the new variety "Honda Rice."

Rice was also part of the story of the American-Vietnamese war. Efforts to help Vietnamese rice farmers overlapped with the American-Vietnamese war. U.S. Army First Lieutenant Thomas R. Hargrove came to Chương Thiện Province in the Mekong Delta in 1969 as an agricultural advisor to the South Vietnamese Army. Chương Thiện Province (now mostly Hậu Giang Province south of Cần Thơ) was a major base for Việt Cộng and one of the most dangerous provinces in the Mekong Delta. But Hargrove was not there to make war against the Việt Cộng. He was there to teach farmers to grow a new variety of rice, IR 3240, in two crops per year. Although Hargrove often feared for his life, he kept working for the Vietnamese farmers. And since rice was such an important part of the Vietnamese food supply, and the varieties that were planted in the South might be useful in the North, the Việt Cộng watched his work and left him alone.[7]

After the war and reunification, Vietnam's rice industry struggled. The land had been heavily damaged by war, and the country was suffering in its aftermath. Also, the United States-imposed trade embargo prevented the Vietnamese rice from being exported into many international markets. Vietnam was attempting a centrally planned economic system, but its attempts to collectivize its agriculture was failing, just as it had failed in China and the Soviet Union.

Then, in 1988, Agricultural Minister Tạn led a radical and stimulating discussion at the Vietnamese National Assembly and the state revised its policy. It declared every "farm household to be an independent, self-directed economic unit that has the right to plan and perform its own production and business and to enjoy its results...The potential capacity of tens of millions of farmers can only be fully mobilized for producing more wealth for themselves and society when they become the real owners of their land."[8]

At the same time, IRRI's introduction of new varieties of rice into Vietnam, and specifically the Mekong Delta, dramatically improved yields for the farmers. As of 1993, "IRRI varieties now covered 70% of the irrigated rice-growing area in the Mekong River Delta."[9]

Vietnam was also developing its domestic expertise. Dr. Võ-Tòng Xuân, for instance, was an agronomist who lived in the Mekong Delta. He had been actively involved with IRRI since the 1960s. He was Thomas Hargrove's guide and translator after the war. In addition to working with IRRI, Dr. Xuân was Vice-Rector at the University of Cần Thơ and Director of Mekong Delta Farming Systems Research and Development Centre.

He was known throughout southern Vietnam as Dr. Rice, and he had a popular television show on the one government-controlled station in the delta in which he taught farmers better techniques for growing and cultivating rice.

At an IRRI conference in Hanoi in 1994, Dr. Xuân presented a paper entitled *Vietnam and IRRI: A Partnership in Rice*, which stated that "Vietnam emerged from a state of near famine to become the world's third largest rice exporter after Thailand and the United States. The export of 1.67 million metric tons [MT] of rice [in 1990] was a surprise not only to the international community but also to the Vietnamese." He went on to say, "Although other factors — improved technology, better irrigation systems, and increased availability of inputs — contributed to the big gain in Vietnamese rice exports, the underlying factor was the rapid change in government policy, known as *doi moi* or "Renovation." The changes included the 'privatization' of agriculture, opening of foreign trade, and setting a competitive exchange rate for the Vietnamese đồng."[10]

At the same conference, Mr. Mahabub Hossain, a staff member at IRRI, delivered a paper also pointing out that the change in the Vietnamese government's policies had a huge impact on the growth of the rice industry. "Since 1981, when the political leadership decided to make a transition from central planning to a market-oriented economy, the agricultural sector has grown at 4.1% per year, a performance similar to China's and superior to the 3.4% growth achieved in Asia as a whole."

Mr. Hossain went on: "The main factor behind this impressive agricultural growth has been a vibrant rice sector. Rice production grew at more than 4.7% per year, the highest in Asia and more than double the average [of Asian countries] during this period. Over the last 7 years, the Vietnamese economy has expanded by more than 6.5% per year, a record to be envied by most developing countries of the world, and a sharp contrast to the disastrous performance of similar transitional economies in the former Soviet bloc."[11]

In an additional paper at the conference, Dr. Xuân explained, "As for most governments after a destructive war, food security was the main concern of the Vietnamese government immediately after fighting stopped. Every Vietnamese farmer was encouraged to grow high-yielding rice."[12]

As shown below, the area converted to IRRI rice varieties from 1968 to 1974 was rapid and huge.

Area of IRRI Rice Varieties in South Vietnam 1968–1974

Year	Area (ha)
1968/69	23,373
1969/70	201,000
1970/71	452,100
1971/72	674,740
1972/73	835,000
1973/74	890,400

Source: National Bureau of Statistics, Saigon, 1974.

Taken from Dr. Xuan's 1994 speech: History of Vietnam-IRRI cooperation

The Vietnamese farmers were keen on growing the most advanced rice available and were constantly adopting the latest varieties.

Vietnam now produced three major rice crops a year. And because of that annual productivity, farmers were able to adjust their rice seed varieties quickly and frequently. This rapid adoption by the farmers of new rice varieties also helped the JV. The farmers quickly recognized that the JV was paying for quality. The farmers were willing to quickly change their varieties to achieve higher quality so they could sell their rice to the JV.

From being a net importer of rice in the 1970s and 1980s, Vietnam once again became an exporter. Exports of Vietnamese rice grew from 153,000 MT in 1987 to over 2 million MT in 1995 as shown below.

Source: USDA October 1994 *Rice Situation Report*

The release of the trade embargo by President Clinton offered Vietnam a chance to re-establish itself in the world market. ARI recognized the opportunity to invest in the Vietnamese rice export industry well before the trade embargo ended, and

ARI planned a strategy to enter the market as soon as the embargo was released.

However, the Vietnamese food shortage between 1975 and 1994 resulted in a very conservative approach to opening the market to ARI. Having had many years of starvation, the Vietnamese government was concerned about exporting rice that might be needed to feed the domestic population.

In addition, during the years after unification, the country was desperately poor. While the government was ostensibly a centrally controlled communist government, the reality was that the central government had few financial resources to offer the country's provinces. Consequently, each province had to fend for itself financially.

Since export permits were a source of income, they were carefully controlled at the national and provincial level. The central government granted a limited number of export permits to the two major state-owned rice processors—Vinafood I in the North and Vinafood II in the South. Vinafood II became much larger due to its proximity to the Mekong Delta where most of the Vietnamese rice was grown. In addition, each province was granted a limited number of rice export permits, which were a needed source of income and were controlled carefully by the provinces.

ARI optimistically assumed it could participate in the Vietnamese rice export industry despite the export permit policies. ARI's goal was to produce high-quality rice and export the rice at higher prices than Vietnam had experienced historically. Farmers would benefit, employees in the rice industry would benefit, and Vietnam's balance of payments would benefit. Rice export permits would be needed for ARI, but the benefits would be obvious to everyone. Keep Smiling.

To obtain high-quality rough rice, the JV hired Dr. Xuân to encourage the farmers to grow high-quality rice for which the JV was willing to pay premium prices. The farmers quickly appreciated what the JV was doing—buying quality. Dr. Xuân met with farmers to explain this to them. He instructed them to plant IR64 as the best quality and provided technical support to the farmers.

Dr. Võ-Tòng Xuân advising me about rice quality

6

Living in Trà Nóc and Cần Thơ

Claire and I were like some middle-aged Peace Corps volunteers venturing into the Third World but with a bit more capital in hand. The building we'd chosen in Trà Nóc to live in needed a lot of work. And this was not Saigon. It was a rural and industrial area where foreigners were not expected to live.

We hired some local craftsmen, and we had a bathroom with a Western toilet installed. I had some bamboo furniture made, although like so much else, the design I sketched lost something in the translation. We bought a bed and hung up mosquito netting. A loud but mostly working A/C unit was installed in one window. And Claire brought things from home to make it look more like home.

Outside the "house" was another challenge. It was littered with garbage, both paper and plastic household items, and all the leaves and branches that fall in a jungle area. Claire hired some of the laborers to pick up the trash in the yard so it could be planted. Since we loved birds, we had a lovely wooden and screened aviary built there too. The effort was a success and provided us a nice place to sit outside.

Water was another challenge. Although the Vietnamese are clean, most people lacked a source of water, and they bathed in the river.

Woman bathing in the river

That was not an attractive option for us. Everything went directly into the river, from industrial waste and chemical pollution to garbage to human waste. Drinking water was not available except in soft plastic bottles, which in the heat, added their own toxic smell to the filtered water. So we installed a filtration and disinfecting system for our water source.

It was a a pleasure not to have to use bottled water to brush our teeth and to take a shower without clamping our mouths shut the entire time. The concern about waterborne illness was constant, but we were careful. In the entire time we were in Vietnam, we did not incur any sickness from anything related to food or water.

As luxurious as taking a shower was, it was not always reliable. There were frequent brownouts or power failures, and our water system required electricity. One day when Claire was in the shower, her hair all lathered up, the water stopped. She waited and considered stopping, but she heard some noise outside and decided to look. Our shower had a small window about head high, and she slid the window open and saw a line of women there, just on the other side of the wall.

They all had plastic buckets or dishpans, and they were waiting in line to fill them from our newly installed waterline. They had figured out how to tap into our filtered water and were eager to have access to this source of clean water.

Using a bottle or two to rinse off, Claire went out to find out what the women were doing and later told me how upsetting it was to her. It was not that she was left with shampoo in her eyes but that these women had no access to clean water, and until then she did not know it. It just had not occurred to us. So Claire asked that the JV expand our system to provide for both them and us, and our clean water was restored.

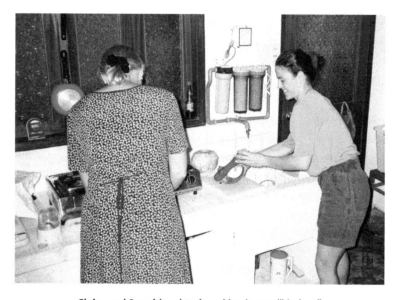

Claire and Sara (daughter) cooking in our "kitchen"

As to the kitchen, well, there was no such thing anyway. Most of the cooking was done outside on small stoves and grills, and the washing up was just a plastic tub. We did not hire a cook— we were assigned one by the factory. After all, there were no grocery stores and no way for us to buy food, so the woman who was assigned to us, a part-Cambodian woman by the single name of Ut, would shop and cook. Sort of. Her repertoire was extremely limited because she was not a cook. Her previous job was to serve tea in the office building. But she did grill fresh shrimp, cook rice that was mostly bug free, and buy the wonderful fruit we loved at the market in Cần Thơ. She made an Asian pesto that we devoured, with basil and garlic which we enjoyed so much we brought some home to California.

We traveled back and forth from Trà Nóc to Saigon regularly so that we could maintain our sanity by experiencing hotel food and our special treat, Haagen-Dazs coffee ice cream, and by watching the one English language television station that announced, with the inimitable voice of James Earl Jones, "This is CNN International."

Mainly, we loved to get our hands on the *International Herald Tribune* (IHT). We asked the Omni Hotel to save up copies for us, up to a month's worth, and when we arrived, they had them ready for us. We went right to Dave Barry's column for some much-needed humor, and Calvin and Hobbes saved our sanity many times. Then Claire would take a few copies with us to savor when we returned to Trà Nóc. She could make one issue of the IHT last for a week by only reading one or two pages a day with her morning tea.

Traveling back and forth was a challenge, as the only vehicle available initially was an older model VW bus. Since we didn't leave Trà Nóc until 5 or 6 p.m. on Fridays, we would take naps in the VW stretched out on the hard, barely padded bench seats. Fortunately, we had a good driver, Chung. And when we finally were able to buy a new car, and chose a Toyota Land Cruiser, he was ecstatic. As were we.

Claire's major contribution to our comfort was talking Chung into only using the horn when absolutely needed. Chung was a reliable and knowledgeable driver on the roads, but he didn't tolerate slower cars, motorcycles, bicycles, or pedestrians very well. He had a great sense of humor, and we all had a laugh when he pointed to a reckless motorcycle driver and said "Muốn chết!" or in English that the person "wants to die."

I remember late one Friday night when he drove me to Saigon. As was the case when traveling alone, I slept in the front seat. I woke due to some severe bouncing of the car. I looked up and noticed that he was driving on the shoulder on the wrong side of the road.

But hiring good people to work for us was not simple because of the legacy of the war. As I began to look for persons to add to the rice facility's employees, I was told in clear terms that I was not to hire persons who were on the "wrong side of the war." However, that was a challenge because they were the ones who spoke English. Hiring translators was a special challenge because the only ones available in Cần Thơ learned English at school and had never conversed in English.

Vietnamese is a complex and subtle language of tone and context. Many times, I needed two translators in my meetings so that I'd have a reasonable chance of having the conversations translated accurately. But that also meant that when something was said in Vietnamese, the translators would take several minutes discussing what it meant before offering me an English version. That slowed many already interminable meetings down considerably.

In our first year, I was immersed in getting the rice mill cleaned and functioning. Meanwhile, Claire took on another challenge. She had a background and interest in organic farming, and as a strong environmental activist, she was concerned about the amount of pesticides and industrial chemicals being used on local farms and the amount of pollution in the river and canals. She decided to start a demonstration organic farm to grow food without chemicals and provide a model of clean farming for the local village women. She'd learned they were bringing highly toxic weed killers home from the rice fields to use on their "kitchen gardens." And she learned from Dr. Xuân that there were no labels or instructions for them to use the pesticides safely.

She took over empty land next to the buildings in the rice facility to plant an organic farm. She went to a nearby farm and hired a water buffalo to clear the land for planting, which became the Sông Hậu Organic Farm. She also found a young man to help whose name was Sang.

Sang was one who the government considered "on the wrong side." He had poor prospects for employment. He had tried to leave Vietnam on a boat but was forced to come back and be "reeducated." And like all those who tried to leave, he was not considered employable. But since Claire was just hiring him for "personal" work, we ignored the rules, and under Sang's care, the farm flourished—eventually.

Sông Hậu Organic Farm

It took almost a year, even with Vietnam's two growing seasons, to learn how to source organic fertilizers (from local animals). She also had to learn which crops grew well in the tropical climate without the use of toxic chemicals. There were many trials and many failures. Claire would complain that the grasshoppers were the size of tanks, and she faced constant crop losses. She consulted local farmers and finally things grew well. Claire worked with Cần Thơ University and some international nongovernmental organizations (NGOs) to create a beautiful demonstration farm for local women to show them about growing food for their families without poisons.

She would harvest food, put on a lavish lunch for local women, and then take them on a tour of the farm to demonstrate how it was done—all with translators, of course. And the produce was something we enjoyed, as it rounded out our usual diet of shrimp, rice, and fruit.

Claire hosted a lunch using produce from the farm

I also entertained the JV managers and visitors—particularly rice farmers. In Cần Thơ, the Ninh Kiều restaurant had a long table outside, at which we could seat twenty to thirty persons. We hosted many dinners with lots of speeches and toasts. Our translators worked hard to keep up with the alcohol-fueled toasts. At one dinner, an old farmer stood up, swayed a bit, held up his glass, and said to me, "I want to welcome the American to my country. We had a war with you not long ago. And if I had seen you then, I would have shot you. But now, here you are. So I will let you buy my rice."

After our dinners in Cần Thơ, we returned to our house in Trà Nóc in a motorized cyclo for the 11 km trip.

Claire and I enjoying a cyclo ride back to Trà Nóc

It was usually a warm tropical night, and the trip was a chance for us to be alone. But privacy was never an option, not just because the people lived so closely but also because we were followed and watched as a matter of routine. That got old after a while. We thought maybe the living quarters were bugged, so we found ways to talk about things, like our kids, in our own language. Even if we were having a disagreement, we'd use code words and then crack up at the idea that what we were saying would make absolutely no sense to anyone else who might be listening to us.

We learned very quickly to empty our shoes before putting them on. And we eventually got used to the morning broadcasts over the loudspeakers of the Vietnamese propaganda for the day.

We knew, going into this, that we had much to learn. It was part of what made living in Vietnam, particularly in the Mekong Delta, exhausting. There was the work we were there to do; the living arrangement; the constant cultural interactions that may or may not have gone well; and the pressure to represent ourselves, American Rice, and our country.

But living in Vietnam was never boring. After a long, hot, sweltering day, Claire and I walked through the rice facility down to the river to sit on the dock. We'd watch the river traffic and the locals bathing (fully clothed), playing, and laughing nearby. We talked about our day and hoped to catch an evening breeze. People came next to us and sat down. We did our best to communicate with gestures and laughter. Their friendliness and evident effort to communicate was touching. There was always the possibility of misunderstanding, but a sincere effort to be kind never needed translation.

Keep Smiling!

7

Hanoi

After the first year, I had to spend more time in Hanoi. The differences between Saigon and Hanoi were stunning and dated back over one hundred years. It was said that in "Saigon you exist, in Hanoi you live."[13]

Saigon was and still is the commercial capital of Vietnam. While I was there, most of the architecture was very unimpressive. There were still some remnants of Saigon's colonial and wartime past, but as the city grew, it built more of the drab skyscrapers. However, Saigon's street life was vibrant, spilling out of the shop doors onto the sidewalks and into the streets.

However, what really set Hanoi apart was the restored and still vibrant French colonial architecture. The city took care to preserve its architectural past, from an opera house that was a duplicate of one in Paris to its historical shopping areas devoted to cafés, crafts, and art. Many of the original French houses were upgraded to their original condition because there were so many diplomats living in Hanoi whose organizations could afford to maintain them. Sometimes I took a taxi around the neighborhoods just to admire the houses, and I spent many evenings on long walks around the beautiful Hoàn Kiếm Lake. As the nation's capital, Hanoi seemed more adept at combining modern growth with historic preservation.

The Old Quarter of Hanoi was a charming center of specialized little shops. Over 200 years ago, it was the residential, manufacturing, and commercial center, where each street was specialized in one specific type of manufacturing or commerce.

Craftsmen from villages around Hanoi would gather on the street, which was specific to their guild, and sell their wares to merchants. The crafts or guilds became the street name of the quarter so that most streets acquired names starting with "hàng" (wares), such as Hàng Tre Street (bamboo wares street) and Hàng Dong Street (copper wares street). It was still the practice of street vendors to carry their products in two baskets balanced on a stick that was placed over one shoulder.

Inevitably, change and growth brought new street ordinances intended to clean up the clutter. Vendors were no longer allowed to set up shop on the sidewalk anymore. It freed up the sidewalks, but it was hard on the vendors. They would operate their soup business as usual, with customers sitting on small plastic stools outside, then a policeman would come down the street, and everyone would quickly pack up and disappear. Ten minutes later they were back in business.

The economics of the soup business was more impressive than I thought. A soup vendor sold 100 bowls per day of rice noodles at 2,000 đồng per bowl—or 200,000 đồng per day. The whole family worked together making the noodles, washing the noodles, and making the soup.

I was told the cost of ingredients per bowl was about 1,000 đồng. So the family could make an impressive 100,000 đồng or about $10 per day.[14]

The reason I spent so much time in Hanoi was to meet with Vietnamese and U.S. government officials. The more difficulties the JV faced, the more trips to Hanoi were required. And the more frustration I felt.

I had one rare moment of serenity sitting at the "Long Bar" in the historic Metropole Hotel. I was chatting with Ken Moorefield, the first U.S. commercial counselor. Although his prediction about my chances of persuading the Vietnamese government to help the JV were grim, the setting made it tolerable. Something about sitting at this long, historic, beautifully built bar made it pleasant to listen to bad news.

Another reason to love Hanoi was that a friend lived there. Brad Babson was the World Bank representative based in Hanoi. He was a Williams College graduate, and since I had attended Amherst College (the colleges were rivals), we had a great reason to socialize together. It became a highlight of my time in Hanoi.

I remember the first time Claire and I met with Brad and his wife, Kitty, at their beautiful house, full of Vietnamese art and their good company. After that visit, Claire looked at me and asked, "Why aren't we living in Hanoi?" I think that she was jesting, but it did make me stop and wonder.

Brad and Kitty Babson, Claire, and me at their house in Hanoi

About that time, both Claire and I were feeling the fatigue of living in the discomfort of the small concrete building in Trà Nóc. But I had so much work to do, I did not feel the discomfort as much as Claire. In the end, we had quite different challenges to face in Vietnam. We both recognized that we were not the typical expats who worked for a company or government and were used to that lifestyle.

8

The Team

The first challenge was negotiating the Joint Venture Agreement and obtaining the license from the State Committee for Cooperation Investments (SCCI). Then I had to develop a management team that could update and operate the Trà Nóc facility. I had the benefit of bringing Bill Bond and Kevin (Kiệt) Nguyễn from the U.S. to help.

Bill became the production manager of the joint venture because of his experience at ARI.

Bill Bond, an Iranian rice inspector, and me

Kiệt became the chief accountant because of his accounting degree and his ability to speak the Vietnamese language.

The Trà Nóc facility had been operating prior to the JV being formed, so there was already a full Vietnamese team on-site. My counterpart in the JV was a representative from VF, Deputy Managing Director Phan Văn Tạn (known as Muoi Tạn). He had been the managing director of the facility before I came, so I was uneasy about how he would take to my role as general manager and his boss. I suspected there would be some resentment on his part because he was now number two in the management team. These organizational rearrangements are never easy in any business operation.

Muoi Tạn, Kiệt Nguyễn, and me

Other key JV managers were Quang Thành, who led the rough-rice purchasing team, and his wife Bích Liên, who oversaw the administrative functions. Both were entrepreneurs and had founded businesses of their own. Thành was particularly experienced in rough-rice purchasing, as he had his own rice mill. And Bích Liên was one of my most trusted and effective managers.

Quang Thành and Bích Liên with Minister Tạn

Minister Tạn made frequent trips to Trà Nóc. He was always comfortable chatting with the workers at the facility, and the workers in turn were relaxed when talking with Minister Tạn.

Minister Tạn visiting with workers at the Trà Nóc facility

The rest of the management consisted of nineteen managers responsible for all nine processing buildings, shipping, QC, HR, environmental, and of course the Communist Party.

The JV organizational chart on the next page shows how many managers worked at the JV. This top-heavy structure was a fact of life in a state-owned enterprise.

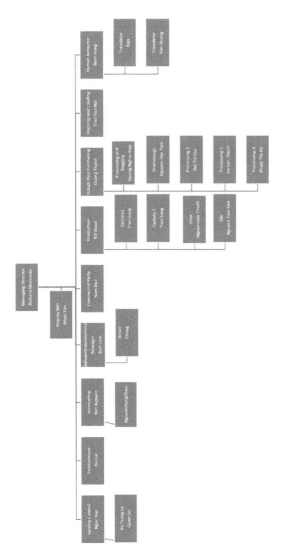

Organization chart of JV managers

Some of the managers of American Rice-Vinafood JV

The JV offices were in a two-story building inside the rice facility. The first floor was used by the production and accounting team. The second floor was used by me, the Communist Party meeting hall, and the quality assurance labs.

My office had a long conference table so that all the managers could sit together in our meetings. The Communist Party meeting hall was quite impressive, considering it was only used one afternoon per week.

Communist Party meeting hall

When I began to face the challenges of starting the joint venture, I knew that I had three major problems:

- I knew nothing about Vietnam.
- I knew nothing about how to ship rice (or any other product) out of Vietnam.
- I didn't speak the language.

Naturally, my first task was to hire someone who could help me with all three problems. Early on, I sought the advice of expats that were already living in Saigon. Dam Pederson of the East Asiatic Company, a Danish company, recommended that I interview a woman named Lâm Hoàng Oanh. Oanh had worked with him in shipping and logistics.

I met with Oanh in a café in Saigon. Her English was excellent, and she knew a lot about export shipping. Then, when I looked at her CV, I noticed that she was born on April 23, 1946. Considering that Vietnam time zone was fourteen hours ahead of California time zone, I realized that her birthday was the exact same date as mine, which was April 22, 1946, in the U.S. What are the odds that I was halfway across the world and I met someone with the same date of birth as me? I hired Oanh on the spot.

Oanh's personal story was fascinating and not unusual for Vietnam. Her father had joined the army in the North during the war with the French. Oanh never saw her father very much. In fact, she says she only saw her father once or twice during the French occupation of Vietnam. During the American-Vietnamese war, he was a high-ranking officer fighting for the North. She explained that every family had extended relatives on all sides of every conflict. "Every family had a story" about who joined which side, she explained.

Oanh worked for a civilian agency in logistics at Tân Sơn Nhất International Airport during the American-Vietnamese war. She was an excellent English speaker and very experienced in logistics. When the war finished, she was one of the few English speakers who stayed in Vietnam. Most of her associates left Vietnam for fear of reprisals.

But Oanh stayed and lived through the subsequent challenging economic times. Even though she'd worked for a company that had helped the U.S. during the war, a position that often resulted in being blackballed, her skills had resulted in her being hired to work for the largest import/export company owned by the Ministry of Trade under the new unified Vietnam. As she explained it, there were very few persons left who could speak English. They needed her but didn't necessarily trust her. And it was Oanh's ability to thread all those obstacles that made her invaluable to me and the JV.

Oanh and me

Oanh became my advisor on all things relative to Vietnamese law and shipping practices. Her first job was to find an office for American Rice (V.N.) Ltd, the representative company which we formed, as allowed by Vietnamese law. Then, as soon as the JV started shipping, she managed the shipping documents, fought with the vessel captains to assure loading speed, made sure all documents were submitted for customs clearance, and made sure that the letters of credit (L/C) were documented correctly. For the L/C's, every *i* had to have the dot directly lined up, and all the letters t had to have a dash in the perfect place. In between these jobs, she was translating written communications and verbal conversations with the staff at the JV and with the JV board of directors.

Another valuable member of the team was Trần Văn Liêng. Liêng was hired by Vinafood II as an international assistant to Madame Triều. His job included written and oral interpretation, cargo warehouse inspecting, and shipping, as well as traveling to many countries as an escort and language assistant with Vinafood II management people and with Minister Nguyễn Công Tạn.

Later, when I left Vietnam, Liêng took over as managing director of the joint venture. He had the difficult job of closing the JV and liquidating the remaining 30,000 MT of inventory to pay off the last bank debts, which he did successfully.

Oanh, Kiệt, Ambassador Peterson, me, and Liêng

9

Bank Credit

As the CFO of American Rice, I had established a maximum capital investment of $1 million cash in the American Rice-Vinafood Joint Venture. By the time we had reached an agreement with VF, ARI had committed $3 million, which was still a small amount for a business that expected to have sales of $60–70 million.

I knew I would need commercial banks to provide sufficient credit lines to purchase the rice, to hold the inventory, and then to sell the product under letters of credit (L/C). Often the L/Cs had clauses saying no payment would be made until the shipments arrived at their destination. A typical shipment of rice was worth over $4 million, so having ample credit lines was critical.

As soon as we received our license, I immediately started talking to banks. None of the Vietnamese banks were willing to loan money to the JV, probably due to the lack of familiarity with U.S. companies. The foreign banks had just begun establishing themselves in Vietnam, and they were keen to broaden their visibility. One bank, Standard Chartered Bank, had just set up its office in Vietnam and thought that loans to the rice industry would create a positive and visible impression with the Vietnamese government.

Because over 75% of the population was working in the rice industry in some form, supporting the rice industry was important to the government. And since the JV was managed by ARI, Standard Chartered Bank believed that the JV business practices would be more consistent with Western standards. The bank's country manager, Ms. Iris Fang, believed that with American Rice's reputation and experience in producing high-quality rice, the JV would improve Vietnam's poor reputation in the world market. Presumably, that would even improve the balance of payments. Ms. Fang's interest in our JV resulted in Standard Chartered Bank becoming our first lender.

Her decision to provide the first credit line to the JV required her to get approval from the Asian Board of Directors of Standard Chartered. The chairman was David Moir, a Scotsman who had pioneered his career in Africa.

Ms. Fang had agreed to open the country office in Vietnam after Mr. Moir had suggested it. It was a totally new experience compared to her other assignments. But it had one advantage. Her husband (Andy) had grown up in Vietnam. In fact, Andy's great-grandfather had been part of the royal family of Vietnam.

Standard Chartered's Iris Fang, her team and me

Ms. Fang's analysis was that the credit risk was primarily a delivery risk. Ms. Fang believed that since the shipments were all done under letters of credit, the delivery risk occurred while transporting the rice to the port. And the Trà Nóc facility was over 200 km away from the primary shipping port in Saigon. So the delivery risk was high. Her operations manager, Mr. Eng, had a lot of experience in transportation. Ms. Fang instructed Mr. Eng to study how the JV handled the shipments of rice from Trà Nóc to the port of Saigon to understand how this risk was managed.

The finished rice was loaded into sacks at the Trà Nóc warehouses and then barged from the Trà Nóc dock. It would take three days to deliver the rice from Trà Nóc to the port of Saigon, except in the rainy season, when it would take five to six days due to delays in loading and unloading. Since the rice had to be ready to load onto the ship as soon as the ship cleared customs, the rice was delivered to the port before the ship arrived and was stored in warehouses.

As a result of Standard Chartered's early support for the JV, we subsequently were able to develop lines of credit with Crédit Lyonnais, BNP, ABN AMRO, BFCE, and ANZ. I approached Citibank's in-country officer, Bradley LaLonde, who made numerous trips to Trà Nóc as part of his due diligence. It was clear that he was in favor of providing a credit line to the JV.

Bradley LaLonde visiting the Trà Nóc facility

But ultimately, he could not persuade Citibank to provide us with a loan. I think the reason was that American Rice would not provide a guarantee to support the loan. ARI would not provide a guarantee because it only owned 55% of the JV. We believed that if Citibank called on the guarantee, they would seek 100% repayment from ARI because it would be difficult for a foreign bank to collect from a Vietnamese state-owned entity. I was never able to fathom how Procter & Gamble or other big U.S. companies were able to meet Citibank's requirements, unless they already had credit lines established in the U.S.

After two years of increasingly larger operations, we still did not have any credit lines from Vietnamese banks. Ms. Trần Thị Thu, Director of Vietcombank in Cần Thơ, came out to visit our factory and watched one of our cargos being loaded, but she still could not be persuaded to make us a loan.

10

Buying Rough Rice

The American Rice-Vinafood Joint Venture did not grow rice. It was a rice-processing and exporting company. American Rice and Vinafood were both rice processors. We had to purchase rough (paddy) rice (meaning rice that was right out of the fields and not yet dried or milled) at competitive prices and in sufficient quantity to operate the Trà Nóc facility at capacity levels.

Dr. Võ-Tòng Xuân advised American Rice and the JV on the quality of rough rice purchased.

Doug Murphy, Dr. Xuân, David Kay and John Poole

The Vietnamese government had set up a rough-rice purchasing system which consisted of state-owned companies (SOE) acting as middlemen. These SOEs purchased the rough rice directly from the farmers and then sold it to the state-owned rice processing companies such as Vinafood. Vinafood processed the rough rice and then either exported the rice or sold it domestically.

The JV's license stated that we had to purchase rough rice from these middlemen. Unfortunately, when these companies purchased rough rice from the farmers, they did not pay for quality, and probably cheated the farmers. I soon realized that the JV would not survive if we only bought rice from these middlemen. So I started buying directly from the farmers. I was determined to treat them fairly and pay for quality. Very quickly the local farmers realized this, and within a month, we had thirty to fifty small sampan boats filled with rough rice docked outside our facility each morning.

Sampan boats unloading rice at Trà Nóc facility

Of course, this was illegal under the terms of our JV license. But for some reason, the government did not step in to admonish us. I realized the reason they left us alone much later. It was because Urbain Tran had gone to Hanoi and had talked with Minister of Agriculture Tạn. Urbain explained that the JV's goal was to make the farmers richer and not necessarily to cut out the middlemen. And since Minister Tạn wanted to improve the life of the farmers, as did we, he allowed this practice to continue. Such was the way things worked: not always by the book but always in the interest of Vietnam. If that helped the JV, fine, but it was never a primary point for the Vietnamese officials who were always there watching every move we made behind the scenes.

We needed to acquire large quantities of rough rice to meet our sales commitments. Word was spreading quickly that the JV was paying higher prices for higher quality. It occurred to me that we could also offer incentives for farmers to deliver larger quantities. I remembered how U.S. banks used to offer gifts to new customers who opened an account with the bank. So we set up a reward system that gave prizes to farmers for delivering larger quantities.

Congratulating a rice farmer for delivering 10 MT of rice to JV

I always enjoyed sitting in the JV buyers' office at the rice mill and watching the farmers as they brought their rice to sell to us. They were the most industrious people in the country, and they usually came with their whole families. It was a pleasure to watch them collect payments for their rice.

Rice family holding payments for the rice they sold to the JV

On one occasion, I met a tall older gentleman wearing the usual outfit of black pajamas (his were exceptionally clean and pressed). He had a full head of silver-grey hair combed straight back and a very regal aura about him. He moved gracefully as he walked barefoot from our buyers' office to the cashier to receive his money. I greeted him with "xin chào" (the polite version of hello in Vietnamese), and he shook my hand firmly with both of his and replied with the same. I was struck by the dignity of this old farmer who was probably as poor as I could imagine but who had such pride and self-respect.

From then on, I would notice that many Vietnamese, who were very fastidious about their clothing, were often barefoot. And their feet were wider and larger than those persons who had grown up wearing shoes. At a fancy event in Saigon once, Claire noticed a successful rice farmer wearing a handmade suit, white shirt, and tie (looking as dignified as the rest of the attendees) who was barefoot. We were to learn that for these men, they felt it was more comfortable, and Claire thought that it was perhaps a mark of pride that they continued this practice.

On another occasion when I sat in the buyers' office, a family had come to the Trà Nóc facility with their rice. The mother stood outside the office while the daughter and her two younger brothers did all the negotiating. The mother just looked at us through the window. The "window" had no glass, it was just an iron grate. The mother had both hands firmly wrapped around the iron bars as she observed everything that occurred inside. She was old, thin, and had this look about her that showed a lot of history—good and bad.

The rough rice they'd brought to sell to us had a high level of moisture, almost 20%. When we bought rice above 14% moisture—the desired moisture for milling—our practice was to deduct 1.2% from the price for every 1% moisture above 14%. This was necessary because of the cost of drying the rice to the desired moisture level for milling.

Prices had been dropping rapidly, so we had tightened up our buying practices to slow our purchases until prices settled down. The buyers were under strict orders not to buy any rice over 18% moisture. But this family's rice was good quality.

The JV buyer looked at me to make sure that I agreed that we didn't want to buy their rice. I said nothing, and the buyer told the daughter that we weren't buying rice over 18% moisture. The daughter then caucused outside with her mother. The daughter came back and again asked us to buy the rice. Again, the buyer refused. After one more family consultation outside the office, the daughter came in again to sell us the rice.

I told them (through the interpreter) that they had good quality rice and that they should dry the rice and then bring it back tomorrow. But the daughter replied that rice prices were dropping so fast that they worried that tomorrow's prices would be much lower. During these discussions, the mother never said a word to any one of us in the building.

Finally, I told our buyer to offer to buy their rice if they accepted a 1.4% deduction for each 1% moisture over 14%. The daughter and mother quickly conferred outside. There was a lot of looking over their shoulders as they tried to figure out who I was and how I was involved. Finally, the daughter came in and accepted our offer. I then went over to the window and shook the mother's hand through the window grating. She beamed a big toothless smile. She had obviously been the ultimate decision maker, and she loved the attention I had given her. By then I had learned that in Vietnamese families, it was the woman who oversaw the money. I loved being able to engage with her, but that moment came at a cost. It became the joke around the buyers' office that I was a soft touch.

Rough rice was delivered to the Trà Nóc facility in large boats that held up to 4 MT of rice either in jute bags or bulk. Or the rough rice was delivered in small sampans that held up to 30 bags, or about 1.5 MT. After purchasing the rice, it was un-loaded, weighed, and dried before it was milled.

We had a dock for the larger boats, which often had the rice in bulk. We could either bag the rice right there, load the rice in baskets, or vacuum the rice into our trailers. But the small-er boats would land on the beach, put down a wooden plank from the boat to the beach, and off-load the bags of rough rice over their shoulders.

Rough-rice deliveries to JV docks in larger boats

Unloading rice was a major operation and involved numerous male and female laborers who would carry very heavy bags long distances from the boats to the weigh stations and then to the concrete pads that were used for outdoor drying.

Rough rice unloaded by the female and male stevedores

The drying process was crucial to maintaining rice quality because if the rice was too moist, it would fracture. Although the Trà Nóc facility had an expensive drying facility, donated by the French ten years prior, it was much cheaper to dry the rice manually by spreading it out on the pavement and letting it dry in the sun. It was very labor-intensive, but labor was very cheap.

To dry 50 MT of rice per day, we needed to have fifteen persons spreading rice over the concrete pads around the Trà Nóc facility. And they needed to constantly rake the rice so that the sun could dry it completely.

Solar drying of rough rice

At a large state-owned rice facility in the Mekong Delta, the solar drying area took up the size of five to six football fields.

Solar drying at Co Do State Farm

After solar drying, the dried rough rice was re-bagged in jute bags and hand-carried into the rice-processing buildings. This process of manual drying was incredibly efficient as it rarely created broken rice. When the rough rice arrived at the facility, having been off-loaded in jute bags from the boats or trucks, the moisture content could be as high as 18–20%. Once the drying process was complete, the moisture content was only 14%, which was necessary for processing the rice.

Solar-dried rough rice bagged for carrying into rice mills

Solar drying obviously worked best when the weather was dry and sunny. But in Vietnam, the monsoon season lasted from late April to September, with June and July being especially wet. During this season, the likelihood of rain was about 70%, which meant that seven out of ten days it rained. And those days when it wasn't raining, the humidity was so high that it might as well have been raining.

Monsoon rains were incredibly strong. Water poured from the sky like a fire hose, often hitting the pavement so hard it bounced back up head high. At this time, the rural provinces in Vietnam regularly flooded. Tom Hanks, in the movie *Forest Gump*, described the rain in Vietnam: "One day it started raining, and it didn't quit for four months. We been through every kind of rain there is. Little bitty stingin' rain... and big ol' fat rain. Rain that flew in sideways. And sometimes rain even seemed to come straight up from underneath...."

The population in the Mekong Delta was used to this. Those who lived in the flood plain simply moved from the ground floor up to the second floor of their house. They suspended boards across the water as temporary bridges or just got wet wading through the hip-high water. Roads often had one to two feet of water on them. Motorcycles drove through a foot or so of water, but when cars drove through, if they didn't go slowly, they created large waves that traveled to the sides of the road. The waves flooded anyone or anything along the sides, including the first floors of the homes.

The rain arrived quickly at the rice facility. The women laborers (the drying work was done mainly by women, while the bag hauling was done mainly by men) who were raking the rough rice had to cover the rice quickly. They did it in about five minutes. Think about how you would manually cover a football field with tarps in five minutes. But they did it and did it surprisingly well. Then once the rain passed, they pulled off the tarps, and the raking and drying process began again.

Flooding of roads in the Mekong Delta

Covering the rice during a rainstorm

In the Mekong Delta, farmers grew three crops of rice in one year. The winter-spring crop accounted for about 40% of annual average production. It was harvested in February, and the solar drying was done without much risk of rain. During this period, the JV had 500–1,000 stevedores raking the rice around the 17-hectare facility. Since the buildings and the dock took up about 12 hectares, this meant that solar drying was possible on 5 hectares, or more than seven Vietnamese football fields.

One of the most impressive managers I had at Trà Nóc was a tough-as-nails woman who managed the 500+ stevedores and kept the whole drying process operating smoothly. I didn't let her height fool me for a minute.

Manager of the stevedores

11

Rice Processing

When Gerry Murphy proposed that I go to Vietnam, he knew that I had no experience in rice processing. So why did he feel confident sending me to Vietnam? Maybe he saw in me what I'd always known about myself—that I was willing to learn and adapt. But I had a lot to learn about rice processing.

The Trà Nóc facility was an impressive operation. It had six separate buildings for processing rice plus a building for packaging. The oldest mill was about twenty years old, the newest, about five. Each building had its own ways of solving any milling problems. Take, for instance, rat eradication. While one mill might have traps, even poison, the oldest mill had a pet boa constrictor that did the job. Part of getting the mills to function more efficiently was getting to know all their quirks.

Once the rough rice was dried, it was brought into the milling facilities in jute bags and hand loaded into paddy-cleaning machines, which took out extra straw and other material. Then the paddy rice went through the destoner machines to get rocks and other heavy material out. And finally, it went through a paddy-husking machine where the rough outer husk of the rough rice was removed. At this point it was what is known as "brown rice."

Brown rice was not popular nor sold much in the tropics. The bran was a very nutritious part of the rice hull, but in the tropical humidity, it quickly went rancid. As a result, the white milled rice that was associated with Asian foods was what kept best and was what people preferred.

Next, the brown rice was milled and polished. The best quality rice was polished aggressively to remove all the bran so that the rice had a clean white color. Then the milled rice was sorted by size and broken kernels were separated out as much as possible. The specifications for quality rice were typically a maximum of 5% brokens.

Every Friday afternoon, Ms. Ngọc Hân, the quality control manager, organized a rice inspection and tasting for the managers. Ms. Hân's objective was to continue to seek out high-quality rough rice and make sure it was milled successfully.

Friday afternoon rice sampling and inspection under Ms. Hân's Guidance

The final step introduced by ARI was for the rice to be fed into an optical color scanning sorter. This removed grains that were not completely white. As the rice flowed through the chutes and was exposed to the optical sorter, a camera detected color defects and triggered a compressed air ejector that would shoot out the defect rice.

We installed ARI's optical rice sorters in the newest mill at the factory. It was one of the improvements that VF wanted the most. ARI engineers brought ARI's own optical rice sorters to the Trà Nóc facility and installed them in February 1995. The ARI team had worked in many countries building rice-processing and storage facilities before, so this project was straightforward. And they quickly befriended the Vietnamese.

ARI engineers deployed to Trà Nóc to install equipment

The finished product was then bagged in plastic bags, each weighing 110 lb. Those bags were then hand carried to the shipping warehouses.

No forklifts or other machinery were used to move the rice around the facility. All the rice—whether rough rice delivered to our docks for weighing, or carried to the pavement for solar drying, or carried to the processing mills after solar drying, or carried to the warehouses, or loaded into the barges for delivery to the shipping ports—was carried by the stevedores in bags. I estimated that the rice was carried twelve times in bags between the rough-rice loading dock and the final customer's ship at a total cost of about $1 per day. At times, the JV employed 1,000 stevedores.

During the big spring crop season, the factory ran twenty-four hours per day. As with many businesses, the night shift (midnight to 8 a.m.) was the least productive. I often left my house and walked through the factory in the middle of the night. Initially, I found a lot of the staff sleeping. But before long, they figured me out. The night shift stationed someone outside my house, and when they saw me leave, they ran around and alerted everyone. Consequently I started riding a bicycle around the factory in the middle of the night.

Keep Smiling.

12

Shipping Rice

I began to prepare for our first shipments from the beginning of the JV. Our first crop of rice was the winter-spring crop of 1995. It was harvested in February, and we began buying, drying, and milling the rice immediately.

We also began marketing our rice to some of our customers worldwide. Urbain Tran, in addition to helping establish the JV, was a knowledgeable sales and marketing person. He used his knowledge of the Chinese market to arrange the first sale of 5,000 MT of rice from the JV to China. China had a short crop that year and had to import rice.

Although we believed that we were off to a good start, we quickly came upon an obstacle. When we notified Madame Triều that we were already marketing the JV rice, she informed us that we had strict limits on our export permits. We were only allowed to export 30,000 MT in 1995. In the feasibility study jointly prepared with Vinafood only eight months earlier, the JV had forecasted shipping 120,000 MT in the first year: 1995. If we could only ship 30,000 MT, our first-year operation was going to be a large loss.

The first shipment was loaded in March 1995. It was truly international. The seller was the American-Vietnamese Joint Venture, the buyer was Chinese, and the cargo was carried on a Russian ship. The rest of the year, we shipped to both Indonesia and China.

By the second year, we were committed to proving the JV's benefits to the Vietnamese people. American Rice wanted to demonstrate its technology for producing high-quality rice and selling rice to customers who had not been purchasing rice from Vietnam. We knew we could negotiate higher prices than Vietnam's historical prices, and we knew we could improve shipping technology. The benefit to Vietnamese farmers would be higher income, and the benefit to the Vietnamese government would be a more favorable balance of payments.

Iran was the largest purchaser of high-quality rice in the world. But Iran had stopped purchasing rice from the Vietnamese because of poor quality and defaults on contracts. And yet, in just our second year, American Rice was able to negotiate a contract with the government of Iran for 160,000 MT of rice from Vietnam at prices 20% higher than any prices of other Vietnamese exports. As a U.S. company, American Rice was not allowed to trade with Iran because of an Iranian embargo. But as a Vietnamese joint venture, we could sell rice to Iran.

However, we were only granted export permits for 100,000 MT that year. Again, the JV feasibility study (agreed to by Vinafood) had second-year shipments of 190,000 MT.

Gerry Murphy and I met with Madame Triều to seek additional export permits for the Iranian contract. Unfortunately, it was the day before the beginning of Tết—the Vietnamese New Year—and Madame Triều was anxious to complete the meeting so she could attend to this important holiday.

We met in her office in Saigon. Madame Triều informed us that ARI had to transfer the Iranian contract to Vinafood since the sale was to the Iranian government. It was a government-to-government contract, she said. Gerry politely pointed out that (1) ARI had won the contract due to its reputation in the international rice industry, (2) Iran was not willing to buy from a Vietnamese government-owned company, and (3) Vinafood did not have the equipment or expertise to meet the very strict Iranian standards. The message was not well received.

The contract was for 160,000 MT, and the JV had an annual capacity of over 200,000 MT. However, VF believed that with export permits restricted to 100,00 MT, ARI would have no choice but to transfer the contract to VF. Madame Triều didn't understand that Gerry never gives up, and eventually Madame Triều gave up her request. The meeting lasted over four hours. As I was walking out of the meeting with Gerry, I mentioned that I thought we had "won the battle but lost the war." From then on, Madame Triều was going to make life difficult for us. Rumors were that she was criticized by the government for "losing" the Iranian relationship.

Loading rice into ships in Vietnam traditionally involved tying 30–40 bags of rice together. The rice was then lifted from flat barges and loaded into the ship's hold using a crane and a boom. As can be seen in the picture below, this method was awkward at best and dangerous at worst.

Loading bags of rice at Saigon Port the traditional way

The rice bags were then stacked one by one in the hold of the ship by the laborers. The labor involved was enormous. This was not a problem in Vietnam, as labor was abundant and cheap, but for our international customers, it was expensive. From a safety point of view, it was unacceptable.

We began switching to a much more efficient and safer method utilized by American Rice in the United States. We stacked the rice bags into large slings and then lowered the slings into the ship. This allowed us to load the rice faster and safer. If the ship's cranes could lift it, slings were loaded in two rows with six slings per row. The combined weight in one load was 384 bags or 18 MT. It only took two minutes for the crane to lift the 18 MT from the barge or truck into the hold of the ship. Consequently, a ship carrying 15,000 MT in four holds was loaded in a couple of days, even with plenty of breaks. Normally this took two weeks.

Loading rice in slings

We initially loaded the ships at Cần Thơ Port, but the larger ships used for the Iranian contract were too big for the shallow port in Cần Thơ. We had to take the rice to load into ships at Saigon Port. The JV manager of shipping and loading, Mr. Trần Văn Nại, loaded the bags on barges at the Trà Nóc facility. The barges then traveled to Saigon Port. We stored the rice in a warehouse in Saigon until the ship arrived and was ready to be loaded. The warehouses at Saigon Port were often only accessible by barge.

To load a ship called the *Ploypailin Naree*, the ship's location required the barges to travel from the warehouse along a very shallow part of the river to pull up alongside the ship.

The barges could get stuck in the low water, and we knew that we had to start loading the next day. So, in the middle of the night, hiding from the police, we arranged to have that part of the river dredged so our barges could reach the ship. This was done during the night because it was illegal to dredge the river without permission and obtaining governmental permission might have taken a couple of weeks.

For another shipment, we wanted to load at least a portion of the shipment at our Trà Nóc dock rather than transfer all the rice to the port of Saigon. We could not load all the rice in Trà Nóc because the draft of the river was not deep enough for the larger ships when fully loaded. But we saved a lot of money by loading as much as we could in Trà Nóc.

Unfortunately, Trà Nóc Port had not been used by large ships before. In typical American can-do bravado, the JV's production and shipping manager, Bill Bond, was confident that he could teach the staff at Trà Nóc Port how to load the larger ship.

The problem came when we needed forklifts to unload the slings from the trucks. We rented twelve forklifts to lift the slings off the truck (each sling weighed 1½ MT, so we had crossed the threshold of what stevedores could lift). A caravan of trailers carried the forklifts from Cần Thơ to Trà Nóc. It was the most exciting thing that had happened there since we first arrived.

When the trailers got there, the lead driver turned to Bill Bond and asked where our forklift was to lift their forklifts off the trucks. Bill calmly said, "We don't have any forklifts. That's why we are renting forklifts from you guys!"

Blank stares all around. Then it turned out that even if we got one of their forklifts off the trailer, their forklifts didn't have the capacity to lift the other forklifts off the trailer. So they drove the trailers back to Cần Thơ and had a crane pick up the forklifts and set them on the ground. Then all twelve forklifts rumbled along the road full of crazy traffic all the way back to Trà Nóc, in the night and without any running lights.

After we had converted the shipping to utilizing slings, the ARI engineers told us we should load the rice in bulk. At first, I thought that this wasn't going to work in Trà Nóc, but they persuaded me that the time unloading the rice in Iran would be dramatically less and would save so much money that it was worth the risk. In Iran, they were ecstatic about this, as they saved so much labor by vacuuming the rice out of the ship.

Once we had shipped 100,000 MT under our export permits for that year, we asked the government to provide us with more export permits to complete the Iranian contract of 160,000 MT. They refused. We negotiated with other exporters to use their permits for 40,000 MT. Still, we had to find a permit for another 20,000 MT to complete the contract.

I asked Urbain Tran to purchase Thai rice to complete the contract. It meant paying higher prices, but we knew that American Rice's reputation depended on shipping all the rice agreed to in the contract, even if it meant a financial loss. Madame Triều was not pleased that we had completed the contract without her help.

It was at this point that I realized that the Vietnamese government would never provide enough export quotas to the JV for the

JV to be successful, that is, to operate at a profit. The JV was not allowed to sell rice domestically, so we were boxed in.

Was this an economic conflict or a political conflict? Our partner was a communist state-owned enterprise, so the concept of making a profit was less important to them. And the thought of an American company making a profit from Vietnamese rice might not have been fully understood from the start. The situation came down to free-market corporate capitalism versus Soviet-style communism, and for the latter, power and control were the primary values.

Originally, I had agreed to stay for two years, and by the time the conflict over the export permits had reached its peak, I had been there over three years. It was clear that the JV days were numbered. I decided to turn over management of the JV to the Vinafood team, as required under our JV contract. Mr. Trần Văn Liêng became managing director. I thought Madame Triều probably felt that she had won, but at the same time she acted as if she was sad to see us go. And there was a part of me that was not ready to leave, or to give up on my hope for some success.

13

The *Jenny D*—A True Story

In the first of many ships being loaded for our Iranian contract, we chartered a ship named the *Jenny D*.

I chartered the *Jenny D* from an Iranian broker in Tehran. The ship was over twenty years old and supposedly part of the Dobson line of ships, but in fact it was time-chartered to a Korean company, which specialized in chartering older ships, hoping that the ship could complete "one more voyage" before it broke apart. I know that sentence sounds like the beginning of a Stephen King novel ("a ship sailing toward fog-shrouded cliffs and disaster waiting to happen"), but it was true.

When Tommy Orange, ARI's shipping advisor, first saw the *Jenny D*, he said "This ship could sink with all your cargo in it, and the company would fold up its tent and disappear into the night." It was not a comforting thought. And it was fully reinforced by the captain of the *Jenny D* when he said the ominous words: "This rice cargo is worth about twenty times more than my boat."

The *Jenny D* arrived in Cần Thơ with much fanfare. Cần Thơ is one of those sleepy port towns in which you can make the arrival of a twenty-seven-year old rust bucket a major media event. The "news" was that this was the largest quantity of rice ever to be loaded in Cần Thơ—15,000 MT. The ship could only be loaded with 10,000 MT in Can Tho (still a record) because the river was not deep enough to leave the port once it was loaded with 15,000. The other 5,000 MT would have to be loaded at Saigon Port.

But the Vietnamese press wanted no part of the truth. In all the news articles, the ship's arrival was always described as "a 15,000 MT ship arrived in Cần Thơ today to load the largest quantity of rice ever to be loaded at our port."

The ship arrived on a Friday. It gave a "Notice of Readiness" when it passed the first buoy in the channel entrance to the Mekong River, 30 miles from the port of Cần Thơ. The art of when a Notice of Readiness was sent by an arriving ship was one of those things about which an outsider first learning about ship chartering (me) just shakes his head.

There was nothing remotely connected with truth in the whole process. Ships notified the charterer that they had arrived, even though they were still in the channel, so that the clock started ticking at the earliest possible moment for the pre-negotiated time allowed for loading. The fact that the ship hadn't yet arrived at the port, and in fact hadn't even stopped moving yet, let alone opened their hatches to receive cargo, was a minor technicality.

They wanted to give notice before noon because then we were responsible for loading starting at 1 p.m. that day. For our part, we didn't want the notice to be received until after noon so that we would not have to start loading until 8 a.m. the next day. This timing was also important because under the terms of our charter agreement, we didn't have to load on either Saturday or Sunday if we received notice after noon on Friday. In that way we would have all weekend to inspect the boat and plan our loading logistics (to say nothing about the fact that we had not yet finished putting the rice into bags). According to the ship's log, the ship dropped anchor at 11:50 a.m., but according to the official Cần Thơ Port records, the vessel didn't stop moving until 12:30 p.m. Now you know why we liked the port in Cần Thơ.

On Sunday, when the ship pulled up anchor and began moving to the dock to tie up, it ran aground on a sand bar—not exactly a graceful entrance for all the news media. Fortunately, no journalist covering this event was interested in spoiling a good story with such snags or facts.

The Iranian product inspectors also arrived in Vietnam on that Sunday. We had informed them, our valued customer, that if they wanted to inspect the cargo, they had to be here two weeks earlier. Regardless, upon the inspectors' arrival, they immediately proclaimed that they wanted to inspect all the cargo before any loading began. Since we planned to start loading at 8 a.m. the next day, we decided to keep them in Saigon for the night. Then we picked them up at a leisurely 10 a.m. the next day for the five-hour drive to Cần Thơ. We figured they would arrive about 3 p.m. with the loading in full swing.

We started loading on Monday morning. We were using slings that each held 32 bags and each bag contained 50 kg (110 lb.) of rice. With slings, we loaded faster, and the cargo stayed in better shape during the loading, transportation, and unloading process. We had specially built 28' spreader bars for the slings so that we could pick up 8 slings with a single lift. Thus, instead of loading 30–40 bags, weighing 1.5–2 MT, tied together by a rope and lifting all that into the hatch, we were lifting 12 MT (or over 200 bags) with a single crane. When we had the right kind of trucks, we could pull the slings directly off the truck.

Loading slings onto *Jenny D*

Because of the short time between the signing of the Iranian contract and the first shipment, we had chartered a ship that was not designed for loading slings. This ship had a hatch-cover frame that protruded over the opening of the hatch. The walls of the hatch were about 15 feet inside the hatch. To move the slings underneath the hatch and against the walls of the ship's hold, we had to have forklifts to operate inside the hatches. These forklifts then picked up the slings as they were lowered into the middle of the hatch and stacked them against the walls.

Vietnamese customs officials were always careful about who went aboard a ship. They were strict about requiring boarding passes for anyone to go on board. I guess they were still concerned about Vietnamese stowaways. Nevertheless, per government operating instructions, anything that went aboard the ship must have a boarding pass. The unintended consequence of this policy was that customs required boarding passes for the forklifts.

To have a boarding pass, we had to show that the forklifts had passports. We were finally ready to load at around 11 a.m. after customs officials realized that we could not provide passports for the forklifts. At this point, I should have known that this was going to be an unusual ship loading.

When the Iranian inspectors arrived at our Trà Nóc warehouse, they went into immediate shock at the prospect of having 10,000 MT of cargo already sitting in slings while flatbed trucks were driving back and forth to the port fully loaded. They immediately began inspecting the rice. They expected to reject rice since that was their experience with prior Vietnamese suppliers.

The inspectors ran from one end of our warehouse to the other, jabbed at bags to extract samples, and talked excitedly to each other. One of them let out a whoop when he looked at our scale since it showed the weight of the bag was at the first mark to the right of 50 kg (the bag of rice should weigh at least 50.130 to account for the 50 kg of rice and the 130 gram weight of the bag). After we explained to him that each tick equaled 200 grams not 100 grams, he lowered his voice and ran to the next stack.

They continued this for about an hour. I didn't dare tell them that we were packing product at four other warehouses at the same time. After a couple of hours, I told them that we should go to the ship before loading stopped for the day. We immediately jumped into the car to race to the port. The color drained from their faces when they realized that we were already loading rice on board the ship.

On board the *Jenny D*, the head Iranian inspector took one look inside the hold and immediately began waving his arms and running from hatch to hatch and halting all work. He told me that we should have put dunnage (bamboo mats) on the bottom of each hatch so that the bags wouldn't get dirty. I explained to him that this was one of the benefits of the slings—the slings kept the bags clean. But he wanted no deviation from standard operating procedure. He ran up and down the deck, telling us we had to unload the 300 slings we had already loaded so that we could put dunnage underneath them. It took a while, but finally we convinced him that the slings really would protect the bags.

After about fifteen minutes, we resumed loading. Then he and I watched a sling being lowered into the hatch. One of the slings was lowered directly on top of a small pool of oil which had dripped from one of the forklifts. That was all he needed. He went ballistic. Again, he was waving his arms over his head as he ran up and down the deck, yelling for all the loading to cease. This time he insisted we take out all the slings and put dunnage underneath them.

During an hour of fruitless discussion, he pointed out that (1) this ship was over twenty years old, (2) it wouldn't even be allowed to dock in his country's port, and (3) that the contract forbid us from using any vessel over twenty years old. The inspectors were looking at the wrong contract, but it took another hour to clarify that! By then I was just about to lose it myself.

The joint venture workers had terror-stricken looks on their faces. They feared that they were going to get blamed for this screwup. Then I noticed that the oldest of the three inspectors had quietly disappeared into the captain's cabin, so I joined him so we could talk more quietly.

After a long discussion about the weather and the five-hour ride down from Saigon, I brought up the issue of the dunnage. He rattled off his company's policy. After much longer discussions, I agreed to guarantee in writing that the bottom layer of bags would not be damaged from dirt, oil, or rust. He quietly got up and went to talk to his companions. After another hour, the loading began again.

As they watched the loading of the slings into the hatch and saw how neatly the slings kept all the bags stacked and realized that they would be unloaded the same way—a lot fewer broken bags and faster unloading—they began to breathe easier. Plus, there was something "progressive" about sling loading. It was the very newest and best product-handling system, and we were the only ones using slings for this customer.

But I am getting ahead of myself. Our contract and letter of credit (LC) required us to use the customer's ships for transporting the rice. Unfortunately, their shipping company didn't have any ships available. Even so, we had to have their permission not to use their ships, which as you can imagine in a highly bureaucratic country, took forever to get. By the time we received permission not to use their ships, we had only twenty shipping days to meet our LC contractual commitments. That was why we picked the first (and cheapest) boat we could find—the *Jenny D*.

When the vessel finally did arrive, it looked its age—twenty-seven years old—and had the previously mentioned hatch covers. They were huge steel plates that lay over the holds of the ship. There were four to five covers for each hatch. It took forty-five minutes to close all of them, but I wasn't too concerned. It being March, we were still in the dry season. And it never rains then.

The *Jenny D* was almost filled with the 10,000 MT that we could load in Cần Thơ Port. To complete the 15,000 MT order, we would have to load 5,000 MT in the port of Saigon. That meant that our Trà Nóc team had to finish loading in the big city port. We had done all our prior shipping in Cần Thơ where we were the major shipper, and the port officials did whatever we wanted. We represented about 90% of the total tonnage shipped out of the port. But Saigon was the biggest port in Vietnam. And we knew that sooner or later we would have to ship from there, ready, or not.

As we were finishing loading the *Jenny D* in Cần Thơ, everyone began to look anxiously upwards at the sky, which had suddenly turned a nasty dark color. The captain of the ship came running out of his cabin, yelling frantically, "Rain! Rain! Cover the hatches."

Everybody began closing the hatches as quickly as possible—but not quickly enough. It poured. After we got the hatch covers closed, all we could do was wait until the next morning and see (or smell) how bad the damage was. Anyone who has ever experienced wet rice in the hold of a ship remembers the smell. It is like finding an old pair of dirty sweat socks in your gym bag on Monday because you forgot to empty it on Friday. Suddenly there is this overpowering stench that fills the room.

Wet rice is one of the worst smells in the world. And it will contaminate the rest of the cargo unless it is completely removed. Even though it was the captain's responsibility to pay for any damaged rice (since he was the only one who could make the decision to close the hatches), it would take time to unload any wet rice. And then our employees would have to sort through the rice to throw it away or recondition it.

By sheer luck, the slings had protected the rice from the rain, and none of the rice was wet.

Meanwhile, in Saigon, we unloaded other bags of rice into a warehouse and put them into slings for loading onto the *Jenny D* when it arrived in Saigon Port.

That night I got a frantic call from my assistant, Oanh, who was in Saigon. She told me that the manager of the warehouse was taking out the air conditioner, the desk, and the lights from his office in the middle of the night. When Oanh asked the manager why he was doing this, he said it was just "routine maintenance." I'd seen warehouses in which no furniture was left in the building, and I knew it could only mean one thing—past due taxes!

So, we had 4,000 MT of rice sitting in a warehouse, which was about to be seized by the Vietnamese government tax authority. It was hard to stay calm and keep smiling in the face of these kinds of challenges.

I wasn't about to rely on my legal rights as a "tenant with full rights of occupancy" in Vietnam. At this point we had to get creative about how to get our rice out of the warehouse and back into the barges. So, for a not insignificant sum, we persuaded a crane operator who worked on a nearby construction project to pull off for some "maintenance" to help us out. I didn't sleep very well that night until all the rice was out of the warehouse.

The next afternoon in Cần Thơ, like all other afternoons during our "dry-season" loading of the *Jenny D*, big dark clouds appeared on the horizon. As they moved swiftly towards us, I noticed that the crane for hatch #1 was lying horizontally instead of vertically as would be needed to lift the hatch covers into place. I have never forgotten standing on the deck, watching those dark clouds roll toward us while the crew was feverishly trying to fix the crane.

We had about 1,000 MT loaded into that hatch already, and we were going to lose all of it if the crew didn't get the crane fixed and the hatch covered before it started to rain. When the first mate, who was wearing plastic sunglasses with flamingoes on the frame, cheerily said he would have it fixed in one hour, I almost punched him. I stood on the deck and watched the rain squall literally come within 100 meters of us. It passed by the ship without raining into the open hatch.

That Saturday night, I remember sitting in my house at the rice factory, feeling about as stressed as I have ever felt. The banks were backing away from their commitments to provide us enough money, so we were once again short of cash. The rains came every afternoon, even though it was the wrong time of year. I had another ship coming to Cần Thơ in three days, and I was facing the very real prospect that I would have two ships loading at the same time—one in Cần Thơ and one in Saigon. I was really wondering what I was doing in the middle of a Vietnamese rice factory on a Saturday night.

I finally decided that it couldn't possibly get any worse. Given what I had survived so far, it would only get better, right?

- That was before the Iranian inspector at our warehouse in Saigon discovered 300 MT of rice that had gotten wet in the barge but had been placed in the warehouse.
- And that was before the same inspector discovered that there were a significant number of bags which weighed below the required weight and now wanted us to weigh each bag before we took it out of the warehouse—all 100,000 bags.
- And that was before we learned that our warehouse inspector had not been weighing the bags because he was brand new and didn't know how to use the scale. That went over well with the Iranian inspectors.
- And that was before the stevedores at our Saigon warehouse decided that they were underpaid and needed another 1,000 đồng per MT to keep working.
- And that was before Saigon Port said that the only dock available for the *Jenny D* was at the far end of the

port, which required an extra 20,000 đồng ($1.90) per MT for the barge operators to deliver to the ship.

- And that was before the official notification of which discharge port we were to use came to us on the day the *Jenny D* was to leave. On the notice, the name of the port was misspelled. In order for us to have all of our documents (eight different documents with six originals of each document—all signed and stamped by different government agencies and the captain) be exactly the same as the L/C, we had to have all the documents retyped to match the misspelling.

- And that was before the captain had a heart attack and had to turn over the ship to the first mate—the one with the flamingo sunglasses—to make all the final arrangements just before the Jenny D was to depart...

But the *Jenny D* finally did sail, and the very next day, we started to load the next ship, the *Hậu Giang*. Oanh sent all the *Jenny D* shipping documents to our bank, who reviewed them before they were to be sent by courier to Paris for payment by the L/C opening bank. The documents arrived on a Thursday (naturally, in light of everything else, a bank holiday), and it was not until the following Tuesday that they decided that even though the LC allowed for partial payments, the first shipment of 15,000 MT was a discrepancy from the requirement to have "a 25,000 MT shipment" (singular).

The customer had misplaced the notice. And it was not until Wednesday in London that they sent a request for instructions from their counterpart in the home country. So it was already Thursday in the Middle East, and Thursday and Friday are weekend days in Islamic countries. On Saturday, when they reopened for business, they telexed back to London (who was now on their weekend) to accept the "discrepancy." On Monday, the customer telexed to the bank in Paris that the discrepancy was accepted, but by that time the banks in Vietnam were closed. We didn't collect our funds until Tuesday—six days and over $7,000 in interest expense later.

We only had ten more shipments in this contract to go, and I was sure it would get much easier. At least, during all this time, there were many compensations available in Vietnam, not the least were the fantastic food and the incredible art.

14

Art in Vietnam

On one of my visits to Hanoi, my translator, Ms. Tuan Thị Lê Diễm took me to the Hanoi Fine Arts Museum. Ms. Diễm had studied Vietnamese history and art in college and was a professional tour guide. She was a consultant to Andreas Augustin who wrote the history of the famous Metropole Hotel. In addition to being an expert in Vietnamese art, she became a trusted translator in my meetings with Vietnamese officials in Hanoi.

I was impressed by the art in the Hanoi museum. It struck me as a cross between French Impressionism and Chinese silk paintings. The French clearly had influenced Vietnamese painters during the colonial period, but the artists had maintained their own style as well. Ms. Diễm patiently explained to me why Vietnamese art was so unique.

In 1925 the École des Beaux-Arts de l'Indochine in Hanoi was founded by Mr. Victor Tardieu who studied along with Matisse. The French colonial government of Vietnam had established this school just as they had done in their other colonial territories. The French considered it their duty "to civilize undeveloped, backward, and impoverished regions in Asia," and educating Vietnamese artists was consistent with this attitude. Many Vietnamese artists were sent to study art in France, but Mr. Tardieu also encouraged them to develop their own Vietnamese style.

I loved the artists who worked during this period, including Nguyễn Phan Chánh whose paintings were hauntingly elegant in their delicacy, particularly since they were painted on silk.

Playing 'Go' by Nguyễn Phan Chánh, 1930, ink and gouache on silk

Lacquer painting also provided Vietnamese painters with a unique artistic style. Originally lacquer was used in China and Japan and then in Vietnam.

Lacquer resin is extracted from the sap from lacquer trees that are found in the Phú Thọ Province. The sap is tapped from the trunk of the tree by cutting five to ten horizontal lines on the trunk of a ten-year-old tree and then collecting the greyish-yellow sap that exudes. The sap is then filtered, heat-treated, and colored before it is applied onto a base material that is to be lacquered.

Curing the applied sap requires drying for twelve to twenty-four hours during which the urushiol in the sap polymerizes to form a clear, hard, and waterproof surface. In its liquid state, urushiol can cause extreme rashes, even from vapors. Once hardened, reactions are possible but less common.

Lacquer colors were traditionally three fundamental colors: vermilion, yellow, and black. However, after 1930, new color schemes were developed, which used silvery white, eggshell white, brownish red, blue, and green.

As described in Wikipedia, artistic composition with lacquer materials is known in Vietnamese as "sơn mài." Lacquer can take several months and many coatings to get the desired shine and color. First, a black board is prepared, and thin lines in chalk are picked out with eggshell. Then is it covered with a clear varnish, then polished. Then the layering process begins with colors, then perhaps a silver layer and then another layer of clear lacquer. These colored layers are painted with a brush with clear lacquer layers painted between them. Up to ten layers are each colored, dried, and polished. The finished painting is polished using a fine sandpaper and a mix of charcoal or even human hair to get the right color. In fact, it is not a painting as much as a process that reveals the image beneath.

Summer Wind by Pham Hau, 1940, lacquer

During the August Revolution, which began on August 14, 1945, many Vietnamese artists joined the cause led by Hồ Chí Minh's Việt Minh (the League for the Independence of Vietnam) to fight against the reestablished French colonial rule. For nine years of resistance, the artists' subject matter changed to support Hồ Chí Minh and the communist efforts to resist the French occupation, and images of war and the resistance became common on lacquer.

Reminiscences of a Late Afternoon in Tây Bắc by Phan Ke An, 1955, lacquer

The guide to the museum states that "the presence of the many artworks which used a great variety of media currently on display . . . comprehensively introduce to the viewer the art development with a profound social meaning at the time when our country was under foreign rule and the enemy was adopting an enslaved cultural policy. Despite this, the pioneer painters succeeded in defining the phase of the Vietnamese modern and contemporary painting rich in national character and after the victory of the August Revolution they quickly took off their 'luxury cloak' to join the revolution with works full of optimism. The revolutionary painting of the resistance was formed during the struggle for national liberation and has continued its development up to now."[15]

One of the most famous Vietnamese painters, and my favorite, was Bùi Xuân Phái. Phái studied at the Hanoi College of Fine Arts between 1941 and 1946 and taught there for several years. He was famous for his oil paintings of the Hanoi Old Quarter. He was expelled from the college in 1957 along with many other artists and musicians for supporting the Nhân Văn–Giai Phẩm affair, a movement for political and cultural freedom during the 1950s. The result was that he was not permitted to show his work in public until 1984.

His paintings could still be found while we were in Vietnam. On one of my many trips to Hanoi, I found out that Chris Kreamer, wife of Ross Kreamer who worked at the U.S. Embassy, was also interested in Vietnamese art.

She took on the task of inventorying all the paintings (many of which were by Bùi Xuân Phái) at Café Lam. Café Lam was owned by Nguyễn Van Lam. Mr. Lam had provided coffee, and often loans, to many of the city's impoverished artists during the war. He was frequently repaid by the artists who gave him paintings in return. Rumor had it that he was sitting on an art collection worth a fortune.

After I visited Café Lam many times, Mr. Lam recognized me. He invited me to the café's attic to see all his paintings. I jumped at the chance to purchase one of his paintings by Phái. By then, Phái was widely recognized inside and outside Vietnam. There was always a chance that some of his paintings were copies. In fact, it was often rumored that Mr. Lam's son made some of the copies. So I had Mr. Lam sign the back of the painting he sold to me, saying, "This is the original Phái given by Mr. Phái to me."

Keep Smiling.

Hanoi Street Scene by Bùi Xuân Phái, now hanging in our home

15

Âu Cơ

The Mekong Delta is a water world. And boats are the main mode of transportation. So, within the first year of living in the Mekong Delta, I was determined to be able to explore all the canals and rivers of the delta. To do that, I needed a boat.

The rice factory was situated on the south bank of the massive Sông Hậu River. Because the Sông Hậu was the major route from Cambodia to the ocean and flowed past the JV's Trà Nóc rice facility, as well as the city of Cần Thơ, there was a constant stream of boat traffic of all kinds plying the river.

Some of them were large (and loud) motorized vessels, hauling cargo. Some were small boats, manually operated by hand, with someone standing in back pushing and pulling with long oars. By crossing the long oars and pushing them rhythmically through the water, they were able to move smoothly and quickly across the water.

I tried rowing a boat, but I was never able to get the hang of it. I could not coordinate my two arms and still stand upright on a rocking boat. When I saw a five-year-old rowing her siblings across the river like that, I was impressed.

I am rowing with my passenger holding on for dear life

For my own boat, I was not interested in a traditional rowboat, and a sailboat or kayak was not very practical or even possible to use to get up the narrow canals.

I noticed a long, narrow wooden boat that did not draw much more than a few inches of water and that was both beautiful and practical. It was the traditional kind of boat they used for traveling up the canals. It was about 25 feet long, but only 18 inches wide. Due to its length, it could "comfortably" carry five to six persons—unless all five persons leaned to one side of the boat at the same time.

The boat had a four-foot, long-tailed, outboard motor. The motor was not too strong—it was a five-horsepower, air-cooled engine—and like most single-stroke engines, it made quite a bit of noise. There was never any doubt that people could hear me coming when I was traveling up the river.

To start the motor, I had to pivot the four-foot-long propeller shaft up out of the water and then pull the cord. No one came close to me when I started the motor. In fact, passengers looked back at me with a certain expression that crossed between fear and shock about traveling onto the river in such a strange looking boat and with a seemingly incompetent helmsman. My swearing while trying to start the motor probably didn't help the situation either. I later learned that this kind of boat was called a "Dragon Boat" for good reason.

Anyway, I had decided that this was the boat that I wanted. I found a company that built these boats located about 30 km from our Trà Nóc facility. After negotiating the purchase and a few trips to the boatyard to observe the construction, I was informed that it was time to paint the boat. I wanted the boat to be as traditional as possible, so they suggested painting the boat a light blue. I opted not to have a red-painted bow with a pair of eyes (traditional bow decorations on Vietnamese boats).

The next challenge was naming the boat. Since boats normally have feminine names, Claire, who always liked mythological references, suggested naming it after the first queen of Vietnam, Âu Cơ. According to legends, Âu Cơ was a mountain spirit who married the dragon, Lạc Long Quân, one of the first kings of Lac Viet.[16] Lac Viet was the name of the country that eventually became Vietnam about 2000 BC. And so, disregarding the inference that perhaps a spirit queen had married a dragon, I named my boat *Âu Cơ*.

Âu Cơ at boatyard ready for launching

When I got word that the boat was ready to launch, I traveled to the boatyard and took ownership. I was told that if I traveled east on the river, I would come to Cần Thơ, and from there it would be easy to find Trà Nóc. I left the boatyard about 2 p.m. and expected the trip to take two hours. By 6 p.m., when I had not returned, Claire called the JV management and asked them to find me. I had forgotten my mobile phone, so there was no way to contact me to make sure I was ok. Bill Bond was about to hire a motorboat to search the canals for me when I finally showed up at the Trà Nóc facility. There was a lot of relief at my arrival.

We took many visitors and our daughter Sara on her visit to Vietnam up the canals and Mekong tributaries. Many of these canals were irrigation channels dug by the French in the early 1900s to irrigate their plantations and transport their crops. I really enjoyed the opportunity to travel into the backcountry, and we saw parts of Vietnam that were inaccessible by automobiles.

Traveling up the canals with family in Âu Cơ

16

Vietnamese Food

One of the most popular and unique foods in Vietnam is a soup that is called phở. It comes in two major flavors—Phở Gà (Chicken Phở) and Phở Bò (Beef Phở). Phở is also popular in the U.S. and elsewhere and is my favorite Vietnamese food.

No one really knows where the name "phở" originated. But the Vietnamese believe that it was originally produced in Vân Cù Village in Nam Định Province. Supposedly, it was created by impoverished villagers and then delivered to Hanoi and sold on the streets to both rich and poor people. The evidence for this story was that some of the best phở chefs still come from Vân Cù Village.[17]

Originally, phở was made with beef, but around 1945, some chefs made phở with chicken, and now both are popular. More restaurants served Phở Bò than Phở Gà. But my preference was for Phở Gà as I found it lighter, and how could you go wrong with chicken soup?

The ingredients of phở, for either beef broth or chicken broth, are rice noodles, crunchy fried shallots, onions, and ginger, and it is always served with side garnishes of Thai basil, slices of chilies, mung bean sprouts, greens, and lime wedges depending on whether it is made in the North or the South. The spices used in the broth, such as coriander, star anise, or cinnamon depend on the chef. The chicken and the beef are always carefully selected and prepared by the chef.

But when we lived in Trà Nóc, the chickens there were so skinny and malnourished, it was hard to believe that the chickens contributed much, which might explain the popularity of Phở Bò.

The guidebooks said that you should only go to phở restaurants that served either Phở Bò or Phở Gà, but not both. And heaven forbid that the restaurant served anything other than phở. It was amazing how many phở restaurants in Vietnam follow these guidelines. Urbain Tran's wife, Anna, explained to me that the way to tell the quality of the soup in the South was by the clarity of the broth. Clear broth was the best quality because it required more work to strain and to remove the fat and spice residue.

I heard comments about my habit of drinking all the broth after I'd eaten the noodles and the chicken. Apparently, it was customary to leave broth in the bowl. But for me, the broth was the most delicious part and not to be wasted. When I ate Phở Gà with Urbain Tran, he ate all the chicken and noodles, and then he asked for more noodles in the remaining broth.

What I found most interesting was that the phở in Hanoi was so different than the phở in Saigon. And it was even different in Cần Thơ. Phở aficionados claim that only Hanoi has the true phở. Maybe I'm just not that picky. My ideal day, if I was traveling back from Hanoi to Cần Thơ, was having Phở Gà for breakfast in Hanoi, flying back to Saigon, and having Phở Gà for lunch in Saigon. Then, after traveling five hours to Cần Thơ, I had Cần Thơ style Phở Gà for dinner. Life was simple.

My other favorite food was durian—yes, that stinky, smelly fruit that is not permitted in enclosed spaces. Durian is a specialty of Indonesia but is also grown in Vietnam. It is supposedly an aphrodisiac. That might explain its popularity because it is a real challenge to eat.

Durian has a spiny cover. The pulp inside is extremely smelly. It smells like horribly strong cheese mixed with sewage and diesel gasoline. Travel writers have tried to describe the taste and smell of durian for many years but are still nowhere close to describing it.

A 2017 *Popular Science* article said that "researchers sequenced durian's genome to reveal not only the source of its distinctive stench, but also the fact that it shares family ties with cacao—the plant that gives us fragrant joy in the form of chocolate."

Apparently, everything about the fruit is the smell, which it uses to attract primates in the jungle so that its seeds will be dispersed. "But orangutans aren't the only primate that the fruit attracts; the export market of durian is now upwards of $800 million a year, which is nothing to sniff at."[18]

Due to its overpowering smell, Durian has been banned on public transport across Thailand, Japan, and Hong Kong. In Singapore, the fruit is banned across all types of public transportation, and even taxis have signs to let you know they refuse to carry passengers transporting the smelly fruit.

A 2018 *Mental Floss* article listed some of the descriptions for durian fruit:

1. "Comparisons have been made with the civet cat, sewage, stale vomit, onions, and cheese; while one disaffected visitor to Indonesia declared that the eating of the flesh was not much different from having to consume used surgical swabs." —The Oxford Companion to Food

2. "Tastes lightly sweet and deeply musky." —Frommer's Guide to Malaysia

3. "[I]ts odor is best described as pig-sh*t, turpentine and onions, garnished with a gym sock. It can be smelled from yards away." —Richard Sterling, food writer

4. "To eat it seems to be the sacrifice of self-respect." — Bayard Taylor, 19th-century Journalist

5. "To anyone who doesn't like durian it smells like a bunch of dead cats. But as you get to appreciate durian, the smell is not offensive at all. It's attractive. It makes you drool like a mastiff." —Bob Halliday, Bangkok-based food writer

6. "Vomit-flavoured custard." —The Rough Guide to Malaysia, Singapore & Brunei

7. "The smell of rotten eggs is so overwhelming. I suppress a gag reaction as I take a bite." —Robb Walsh, food writer

8. "Like all the good things in Nature ... durian is indescribable. It is meat and drink and an unrivalled delicacy besides, and you may gorge to repletion and never have cause for penitence. It is the one case where Nature has tried her hand at the culinary art and beaten all the CORDON BLEUE out of heaven and earth." —a "good friend" of Edmund J. Banfield, Australian Naturalist, as quoted in Banfield's 1911 book My Tropic Isle

9. "[Has a] sewer-gas overtone." —Maxine E. McBrinn, anthropologist

10. "Like pungent, runny French cheese ... Your breath will smell as if you'd been French kissing your dead grandmother." —Anthony Bourdain, Chef and Host of *Parts Unknown*[19]

Maybe because I didn't have a good sense of smell, I bought fresh durian while in Vietnam. I brought it back to our hotel room only to be told by Claire that I was not even allowed to let it stay on the balcony outside.

When I went back to my Houston, Texas, office on a periodic visit, I brought some durian and put it in the wastebasket of one of my co-workers while he was at lunch. The rest of us in the office sat waiting very inconspicuously to watch what happened when he came back from lunch. Our offices have glass walls, so we saw him walk to his desk, smell something, and then in a panic, come running into the hallway screaming, "Fire, Fire. Call the fire department." It took about ten minutes for the rest of us to stop laughing, much to his astonishment. Then of course, I had to go into his office and bag up the fruit.

17

Political Efforts for the JV

After the first year of the joint venture, it was obvious to me that I had to apply as much pressure to the Vietnamese government as I could. I made so many trips to Hanoi to meet with the Ministry of Planning and Investment, the SCCI, and the Ministry of Agriculture that my Hanoi translator, Ms. Diễm, had to translate my objections and my complaints tirelessly.

There were benefits of being one of the first U.S. business-people in Vietnam in postwar redevelopment, and particularly since I was in the rice industry. Almost every U.S. politician who came to Vietnam wanted to meet me. I always took advantage of these meetings because it was a great opportunity to meet influential people and to press my case to them. I wanted them to include the frustrations that the American Rice Joint Venture was having in Vietnam when they met with Vietnamese officials.

I was invited by Bradley LaLonde of Citibank to sit at the head table at a dinner in Hanoi for former president George H. W. Bush and Barbara Bush. It was a significant honor, so I wanted to take full advantage of the opportunity. I explained our situation in detail to President Bush. It went about as well as could be expected. He listened politely to all I had to say and then resumed his conversation with others at the table.

I also had a chance to make my case with Senator Tom Harkin; Senator John McCain; Deputy Secretary of Agriculture Richard Rominger; Senator Richard Lugar; the World Bank representative, Brad Babson; the IFC representative, Nguyễn Dinh Hung; and the FAO representative Marcel Messier.

Of course, as Ross Kreamer, first director of the U.S. Agricultural Trade Office in Hanoi, told me, "In discussions with Vietnamese ministries, they were always polite, but they usually just talked around it. It was always difficult to get answers. It was never difficult to deliver the message, but there was never any positive change." He said it straight. Nothing came of my efforts to explain our situation to visiting dignitaries, but the encounters were usually enjoyable.

Minister of Agriculture Nguyễn Công Tạn

Gerry Murphy suggested that we show Minister Tạn the strength of the American Rice business in the United States. We invited Minister Tạn and Madame Triều to come to the United States and meet important United States government officials in Washington D.C.

Urbain, Chương, Minister Tạn, me, Claire, and Madame Triều

We arranged meetings with Senator McCain, Senator Lugar, Senator Bond, and officials from the World Bank.

Claire had experience working with American NGOs. She arranged a meeting with the Institute for Agricultural Trade Policy (IATP) who were assisting in the training of Vietnamese agricultural officials. IATP suggested we include visits to American farms as well. And with IATP assistance, the delegation visited small holdings of Black farmers in the south.

During the trip, we also visited Harvard Business School (HBS), as HBS was writing a case study on the American Rice Joint Venture (Appendix 2). As it happened, a Vietnamese member of the Ministry of Agriculture, Cao Đức Phát, was completing his studies for a master's degree in public administration there. Mr. Phát became Minister of Agriculture from 2004 to 2016.

We took the delegation to Houston, Texas, to show them one of American Rice's processing facilities.

As far as I could tell throughout our time in Vietnam, Minister Tạn was a significant supporter of the joint venture. Ross Kreamer had said that Tạn was one of the more enlightened officials, and "there were not many examples of this in the Vietnamese government."

In our tour of the U.S., we visited a Whole Foods Market in Mill Valley, California. Claire expounded on the gorgeous organic food on display only to find out later that they did not believe for a minute that the food was grown without pesticides.

At the end of the trip, Minister Tạn said that the farm visits were his favorite part of the tour since those farmers were more like most Vietnamese famers, and he could relate to them.

Jim Hall

Jim Hall was the first U.S. diplomat stationed in Hanoi. He opened the U.S.-Vietnam liaison office in January 1995. I immediately contacted him to tell him about our situation. As with many of the first diplomats, Jim had served in the American-Vietnamese war.

Jim was supportive of our project and visited the Trà Nóc rice facility a couple of times to understand our situation and to meet with local government officials.

On one of his visits to Trà Nóc, I took him out on my boat, the *Âu Cơ*. He was visibly shaken as we motored up the small canals. He later confessed that the trip reminded him of traveling up these canals during the American-Vietnamese war. Like many returning veterans, those memories came back often.

Jim Hall riding up the canals of the Mekong River in Âu Cơ

Ken Moorefield

I also asked Ken Moorefield to help us. Ken was the first commercial counselor in Hanoi. He would give me advice while sitting at the Long Bar in the Metropole Hotel. Ken was famous for his role during the final U.S. evacuation of Saigon in 1975. As reported in *Time* magazine, "Kenneth Moorefield . . . put the dazed Ambassador Martin on one of the last choppers out, climbed aboard one himself shortly after."[20]

Ken's advice for the joint venture was quite straightforward, although I didn't want to hear it. He said, "The Vietnamese want the visibility of having U.S. companies investing in Vietnam, but they fear losing control. And U.S. companies are unrealistic about what the U.S. government can do for them."

Ross Kreamer

I met Ross Kreamer at Ken Moorefield's suggestion. Ross was the first U.S. director representative of the Department of Agriculture and thus was interested in helping American Rice's Joint Venture in the Vietnamese rice industry. Ross would frequently insert ARI's issues into talking points for U.S. delegations. He tried numerous times to make a difference. After many meetings on our behalf with the Vietnamese government, the message Ross got back was, "It is ok for ARI to be small scale, but it is not ok to be large and successful." And Ross's frequent observation was, "You know something is wrong when they start smiling—or maybe even hear a little laughter."

Cao Đức Phát

I had met Cao Đức Phát at Harvard when the ARI delegation had toured the United States with Minister Tạn. In my meetings later in Hanoi with Mr. Phát, he was very forthcoming. But he was in no position to do anything about ARI JV difficulties.

However, as the Director General of the Ministry of Agriculture and Rural Development, he had recommended liberalizing rice export regulations. When Mr. Phát became Minister of Agriculture, he continued further improvement of policies and regulations in agriculture and rural development.

Brad Babson

Brad Babson was the resident representative of the World Bank regional office in Vietnam and a friend. Brad was always available to listen to my complaints and more than once tried to put in a good word for us. But he was also very realistic that if we were successful, they would want to find ways to co-opt the success, such as pushing for management control.

Pete Peterson

Diplomatic progress continued between the United States and Vietnam after the trade embargo was lifted. In 1997, President Clinton nominated an ambassador.

President Clinton had been facing resistance to this step by many politicians who did not believe that Vietnam had done enough to find the soldiers missing in action (MIA). But American businesses were pressing President Clinton to move forward so that they could begin to invest in this underdeveloped market.

President Clinton selected Congressman Pete Peterson to be the first U.S. ambassador to Vietnam. Congressman Peterson had been an Air Force pilot during the war and had been shot down and imprisoned in the "Hanoi Hilton" (the Vietnamese prison for American soldiers) for six years. Like Senator John McCain, Ambassador Peterson had both a realistic view of Vietnam and some affection for the country. Upon his appointment, Ambassador Peterson said it best: "I may not be the best candidate, but I am probably the only candidate which the Senate will approve."[21]

Upon arriving in Vietnam, Ambassador Peterson said his priority would be to strive for an accounting of the 2,124 American troops still listed as MIA.

The American and Vietnamese newspapers and TV covered the day that Ambassador Peterson arrived in Vietnam with extensive coverage. CNN had the following report on May 9, 1997:

> Ambassador Douglas Pete Peterson—a former prisoner of war in Vietnam—was met at the airport by about 100 well-wishers, including war veterans and business leaders.
>
> "Today we exchange ambassadors, marking the full normalization of diplomatic relations between our two countries," Peterson said. "This is an historical event and the beginning of a new era of constructive relations."
>
> Peterson was gunned down on an almost moonless night in 1966, when his Air Force bomber was struck by an anti-aircraft missile near Hanoi. He was released

from the notorious "Hanoi Hilton" prison in 1973, after more than six years of torture and solitary confinement in a dank prison cell.

Peterson, sixty-one, returns hoping to serve as an example of someone who survived the worst of the Vietnam War. Waving U.S. and Vietnamese flags, the crowd at Hà Nội's Nội Bài airport welcomed the ambassador's message of moving forward from the legacy of war.[22]

I hoped that by appointing an ambassador and taking such a significant political step forward, I would be able to get the audience I needed to overcome the obstacles that the JV was facing.

Ambassador Peterson was very generous with his time. He met with me frequently and visited the Trà Nóc rice facility numerous times. On one of Ambassador Peterson's trips to the South, I arranged a tour of the famous Củ Chi tunnels where the picture below was taken.

Ross and Chris Kreamer; my driver, Chung; me; and Ambassador Peterson

Ambassador Peterson was a significant break from the typical State Department diplomat. He rode a motorcycle around the countryside and met with so many local people that he was recognized everywhere. I don't know how his security detail was able to keep up with him.

His willingness to come back to Vietnam after his treatment in the Hanoi Hilton was representative of how he performed his duties as the first ambassador. He openly engaged with both Vietnamese and Americans and worked tirelessly to represent the best of American intentions to move past the difficult history of the two countries.

18

The Investigation

As a result of the constraint on the JV export permits, particularly with the Iranian contract, I traveled to Hanoi frequently to enlist the aid of the U.S. diplomats who were stationed in Vietnam, as well as visiting U.S. diplomats and anyone in the Vietnamese government who would listen to me.

Sadly, the Vietnamese government had decided that we were a major disruption. They resented the publicity about our situation that made it clear to other foreign investors that the Vietnamese government was not going to be supportive of foreign investment.

As a result, in October 1996, the government ordered the State Inspectorate of the Socialist Republic of Vietnam to probe the JV. The Inspectorate was responsible for investigating large-scale embezzlement and reported directly to the prime minister. This was Vietnam's internal security service, and they had enormous power. Their mandate was to investigate the JV and particularly American Rice. They speculated that ARI was earning extra money from the JV's customers. They investigated all the JV accounts and talked to all the JV managers.

I was naïvely confident because I knew that we had done nothing wrong. I thought this was just a not-so-subtle message from the government to stop complaining. But I underestimated the situation.

The Inspectorate was, justifiably, greatly feared by all Vietnamese. As one of my Vietnamese workers told me in a very frightened voice, "They could take me away, and no one would ever hear from me again."

So, while we knew that we had done nothing wrong, we also realized that the laws were very vague, the Inspectorate's power was unlimited, and the inspectors had no compunctions about intimidating the Vietnamese on our staff. Our workers were very worried that they would just be sent off to prison or that they would be forced to write a "confession."

We did all we could to be squeaky clean, and we cooperated with the investigation completely. We were never sure whether the investigation was initiated by Vinafood because of our major disagreements over the Iranian contract or by one of the Vietnamese ministries who got tired of listening to the U.S. diplomats convey ARI's frustration about the lack of export permits. Regardless of who instigated the investigation, we had to take it very seriously. It didn't matter why an internal security investigation was launched by an autocratic government like Vietnam.

The investigation by the Inspectorate had one minor and two dramatic events. The minor event occurred one day when the local police came to my office and stated that the American flag over our office building was higher than the Vietnamese flag. I literally had to go onto the roof with the police and measure the heights of the two flags.

Flags of Vietnam and U.S. on the JV office building

But there were two other events that were more serious. Bill Bond, the JV's production manager, had his house broken into in the middle of the night. The "burglars" entered his multistory house in Cần Thơ through the roof, sprayed sleeping gas on his two dogs to keep them from barking and stole his laptop and all the company files he had there. Of course, they had access to all our files at our office, but they must have suspected we were hiding something.

The second dramatic event was a midnight visit to my house in Trà Nóc. Several army soldiers arrived unannounced. Fortunately, Claire was away at the time. They came with one of my JV translators whom they had woken and forced to accompany them. I was sure she was frightened.

I sat them at our dining room table. As they began asking questions, which were inconsequential and clearly aimed at intimidation, I offered the solders one of the bananas that was in a bowl in the middle of the table. The youngest soldier reached out to take one but was immediately yelled at by the commanding officer.

Vietnamese soldiers questioning me in my Trà Nóc house at midnight

The investigation gave Vinafood a chance to avoid its responsibility for the JV losses without mentioning the lack of export permits. After about three months, Chief Inspector Ông Lương Cao Khải filed his report. Upon filing the report, the Inspectorate leaked stories to the press about "ARI embezzlement," perhaps to cover their misguided effort, but that was the end of the investigation, and the Vietnamese government did nothing further.

Toward the end of the investigation, Mr. Khải and I had become reasonably good friends, although it was not a real friendship since he could have thrown some of our team in jail at any time. But in one of my last meetings with Mr. Khải, Oanh (acting as translator) and I were talking about how much effort had been spent on the investigation.

Chief Inspector Ông Lương Cao Khải and me

At one point, Mr. Khải asked me what I did to stay in physical shape. I replied that I practiced yoga. Then he acknowledged that he was also practicing yoga. He asked me if I could stand on my head, whereupon I told him that I could stand on my head longer than he could. He accepted the challenge, and while Oanh looked on, barely suppressing her laughter, Mr. Khải and I stood on our heads for about ten minutes. We then called it a draw, stood up, and shook hands.

Keep Smiling.

19

"Too Right, Too Early, Too Bad"

Why did the joint venture between one of the largest and most successful rice companies in the world and the largest rice exporter in Vietnam fail? As the *Wall Street Journal* (WSJ) said, "Of all the U.S. companies that flocked to Vietnam in 1994, few seemed to hold as much promise." This was a dream that was never to be, and the WSJ wanted to cover it.

The WSJ article was on the front page: "The Houston-based rice company [American Rice]—the largest in the U.S.—planned to team up with a local partner to sell Vietnamese rice overseas. With American Rice hungry for supply, and Vietnam desperate for customers, the venture seemed ideal for both sides and for millions of struggling Vietnamese farmers."[23]

Although the joint venture failed, we were not the only one. International newspapers in 1998 were full of articles about U.S. companies either pulling out of Vietnam or suffering huge losses. P&G lost over $30 million and threatened to put its JV into bankruptcy. The Chrysler Corporation terminated plans to build a $189 million automobile assembly plant. The WSJ article pointed out that "U.S. investment has dropped more than 80% since 1996, to $127 million last year. U.S. companies that haven't closed altogether are cutting back their business and pulling out expatriate staff."[24]

But knowing that other companies lost a lot more money than ARI was not very satisfying. At a meeting between Ambassador Peterson and Minister of Planning and Investment Tran Xuân Gia, Minister Gia explained, "Ten years ago, there were no laws in Vietnam related to business investment. Moving from a state-run economy to a free market takes time. After what has happened to the rest of Asia, they [the Vietnamese] are not convinced that capitalism is best for Vietnam. American companies will have to wait."[25]

That summed it up nicely. At least for Vietnam. But not for me. As to why the JV failed, the frequent answer was that the communist government was hesitant about allowing foreign companies to do whatever they wanted. In hindsight, it was just not the right time for a foreign company to be in the rice industry. But it took me a long time to get over the haunting idea that maybe there was something else I could have done that would have saved the situation.

Everyone associated with the JV had explanations for the JV's failure. Madame Triều said, "The JV was not at the right time." She agreed that lots of blood, sweat, and tears had been expended, but it was just too early. The quota system, over which she had some control, prevented the joint venture from exporting rice freely. Twenty years later, in a meeting with me, as if to emphasize her point, she said that the export quota system had finally been terminated in 2005. Regarding the timing, she was right.

Trần Văn Liêng suggested that it was the contradictory expectations of the two partners. Vietnam wanted the JV to expand the Vietnamese rice market into the United States as a second "victory" after the American-Vietnamese war. But ARI obtained a government-to-government contract with Iran, which embarrassed VF, even though Iran was not willing to negotiate with a Vietnamese SOE. The Vietnamese government blocked the JV in a quota system, because without sufficient quota, the JV could not export sufficient high-quality rice to earn a profit.

Ken Moorefield said, "The Vietnamese government feared losing control of its economy. The Đổi Mới dream of replicating what China was doing couldn't happen."

Ross Kreamer said, very succinctly, "ARI was too right, too early, too bad." In discussions with the government ministries, he said that they were always polite, but that they wouldn't comment on the solutions to the JV problems. They would talk around it and then smile.

Ross went on to explain that this was not entirely a central government position. It was also a grassroots decision made by other state-owned rice exporters who feared the competition. Ross did not name Vinafood, the JV's partner, but I believe that Vinafood was unwilling to accept our competition and potential success, and thus they were less than helpful.

I returned in 2019, twenty years after I had left Vietnam, with memories of both the turmoil and the astounding moments of friendship and drama.

I met with Dr. Cù Chí Lợi, Director of Vietnamese Institute of American Studies. He said that the central government in Hanoi (and therefore by definition, Vinafood, which was owned by the government) did not have the authority to distribute export quotas beyond certain levels. Many of the quotas had been distributed to the provinces, and if the JV were to receive more quotas, the quotas would have to come from one or more of the provinces. Those provinces would object since they earned money from their export activities. And, as I had learned the hard way, things happen in Vietnam by consensus at the local level. So even though important officials in Hanoi might have wanted us to succeed, the industry wouldn't, or couldn't, let it happen.

I heard from many knowledgeable persons, but I realized that there was no obvious way for the JV to overcome its difficulties.

From my point of view in 1996, I had two choices: (1) start paying bribes to the ministries and government officials to obtain more export licenses, or (2) request ARI to spend more money to keep the JV operating, even with large losses. The first option was not acceptable to me as a matter of ethics. The second option—one that seemed to have been used by some of the large U.S. companies who did keep going—was not available due to ARI's finances.

By the beginning of 1998, I had exhausted any good will with many who supported this venture, including Claire. So I packed up and left.

I think that the Vietnamese government was still searching for opportunities to expand its economy. It had many models for growth from other "Asian Tigers." For the government to choose one direction meant achieving a consensus, which was difficult to achieve. Each participant in the process had their own agenda and constituents. It must have been a challenging time for the prime minister and the minister of agriculture.

Could there have been a different outcome, and if so, what would the Vietnamese rice industry look like today? I believe that the rice industry—but more importantly, the rice farmers—would be much more sophisticated. When I returned to Vietnam in 2019, I was frequently encouraged to return and restart the JV.

But on reflection, I am both glad and grateful for this extraordinary opportunity. I learned a lot, not the least of which was the understanding that when you are in trouble, Keep Smiling.

20

Expat: Vietnam 1994–1998

By Claire Hope Cummings

You take a lot of baggage with you when you go to Vietnam - one small suitcase, one carry-on, and two thousand pounds of disjunctive emotions napalmed into your brain from a televised war that won't go away.

—Susan Brownmiller

Seeing Vietnam: Encounters of the Road and Heart

When we first arrived, I saw remnants of the war everywhere. Vine-covered concrete bunkers lined the roads, their open window slits still staring back at us. Steel watchtowers stood on the bridges that spanned the canals. There were bladeless bodies of helicopters lying around, awaiting the metal recyclers. Old U.S. Army jeeps were still in use, their doors now painted with the bright yellow star of Vietnam's flag.

Just down the road from where we lived was a rusting PT boat, partially hidden by palms and banana trees, listing to port, still floating in the weedy water. Smoke rising from burning trash piles always felt surreal. And many people in the Mekong Delta were still wearing black pajamas and conical hats. I suppose I was looking for this. I was curious about the lingering impact of the war on the Vietnamese and still wondering what it meant for me.

Soon though, the complexities and challenges of daily life took over, and my preoccupation with the war faded. Life in Vietnam is intense. There's unrelenting heat, torrential rains, oppressive humidity, open sewers, trash-clogged waterways, constant noise, and ceaseless activity. And did I mention the bugs? Everything was at once both fascinating and unfamiliar.

I wanted to be there. I wanted to support Richard, learn, and travel. Vietnam was important to me as an anti-war activist in the 1960s and '70s. I'd raised my family. I'd been working as a public interest lawyer and wanted to use my training and experience to make a contribution. I did not arrive with a plan in mind. But I soon realized what mattered to me most about life in Vietnam.

Richard and I were on our first exploratory trip to Vietnam to see if we could commit to living there. We'd gone down to the rice facility in the delta and were on our way back to Saigon. That drive, which we would take often in the coming years, took six hours of bone-jarring bumping, swerving, and constant honking through chaotic traffic on narrow levy roads plus two ferry rides across Mekong River tributaries.

We were packed into an older model van with a driver, Vinafood executives, government officials, and Urbain Tran, who was not just a good friend, but whose tireless efforts made the impossible look almost easy. On our way back to Saigon, we stopped to board the last ferry, lining up behind all the trucks and busses. (There were very few private cars at the time.) I got out to stretch and went to sit by myself at the edge of the river. I noticed a woman nearby. She had a baby in her arms and a toddler and, as mother's do, I nodded to her in acknowledgment. By the way she moved and held the baby, it was obvious that she was a loving and caring mother. But I was concerned when I saw her dip an old plastic bottle into the brown river water and give it to the baby to drink.

After we loaded back onto the ferry, we all stayed inside the van with the windows closed, counting on the struggling air conditioner to keep up with the stuffiness. I was sitting in back, next to a window, watching the peddlers crowd around, selling candy, gum, cigarettes, and food. I'd been told not to engage with them. In fact, for most of my time in Vietnam, but especially on our first visit there, I was hyperconscious about not making a mistake or doing something that would reflect badly on us. Besides, I was sitting right next to the most important Vietnamese official traveling with us.

Suddenly I heard knocking on the window next to me. It was the woman with the baby. She held the baby up and pushed it towards me, pointing at me, then at the baby, and then knocking on the glass insistently. Her gestures were unmistakable. She wanted me to take the baby. I was unsure what to do. I glanced around the van, but no one else acknowledged what was happening. I felt terrible for the woman. I gave her a regretful look but then put my hand up to cover the side of my face. I felt deeply ashamed.

When we got back to Saigon, I told Richard what happened. He gave me a hug and said, "You do know, don't you, that today is Mother's Day?" No, I'd forgotten. But ever since then I think of her, especially on Mother's Day. And I still ask myself the question that moment posed: what would it take for someone to give up something important to them, something that they dearly love? What illusion or what level of desperation would it take to do that?

That moment also reminded me that I've always been concerned with the lives of women. I'd founded a women's media collective, chaired a county Status of Women Committee, taught women's studies at a local college, and most of my clients in my human rights legal work were women. So it was clear from my first visit that I wanted to do something around the status of women while I was in Vietnam.

Vietnamese women are incredibly hardworking and resourceful. And in Vietnam it's often difficult physical work. At the rice facility where we lived, for instance, the women did all the work of solar drying. They'd empty large heavy bags of rice onto any nearby flat surface, then constantly rake it all day in the hot sun. Then they'd bag it all up at the end of the day or at the first sign of rain.

Everywhere we went, women were hauling large, heavy loads and working long hours. They also were taking care of their homes and families. Those with a college education could work in offices, but they were the exception. Many rural women made their livelihoods with crafts, weaving mats, baskets, hats, or making sticks of incense and countless other items that were offered for sale alongside the roads. Others grew and sold food from their boats at the floating markets. Whatever their work, women were always dressed impeccably and spoke softly. I especially loved how beautiful the young women were in their long white traditional dresses, the áo dài.

Rice planting is also women's work. In the fields, they stand in lines, stooping in unison, as if in a dance, and press each seedling into the mud. As they work, they sing or tell riddles and jokes. It's the traditional way women work together the world over. In countries that have not industrialized their food system, women still do 85% of field labor.

At the same time, right before my eyes, I saw agriculture in Vietnam rapidly changing. The water buffalo was being replaced by the tractor. Human labor was being mechanized. And women were being displaced. A World Bank study I found showed that when machines or salaried work took over from field labor in agriculture, it was men who got those new jobs.

The seasonal flooding common in Vietnam could be disastrous for women by damaging or destroying their homes or depriving them of their livelihoods. Women laborers led precarious lives. They are under constant pressure to feed their children and everyone living on the margins were in constant risk of hunger. I remember a woman who came to the rice mill. All day she'd sit by huge piles of the rice hulls that were tossed out after milling. She spent hours there patiently picking through the hulls, looking for leftover grains of rice to use for food.

Sometimes I'd go down to the river to sit in the cooler air in the evening and watch the women bathe, fully clothed, in the muddy water. It was one of the few times I'd see them laughing and playing. I'd sit nearby on the concrete embankment, and sometimes they'd come sit next to me. And I mean *right* next to me, as is their way, without any space between us. My idea of personal space was not a concept they understood. So I'd nod and smile, and we'd just sit and watch the busy boat parade before us on the river.

I knew I was witnessing a life and a world that was passing. Soon all that hard and all-too-human labor would no longer be needed. But at what cost to the women whose lives depended on it? And what could I do, if anything, that might make a difference? I was not allowed to legitimately work in Vietnam, but I had means and expertise, and the hope that I could make some kind of contribution.

At the same time, I'd started to study rice farming and production. I already had some experience with rice production because my former husband had been a rice farmer, and we'd lived on the rice ranch where he worked in Northern California. Some of the differences were immediately obvious. In the U.S., rice paddies stood empty. All the work of planting and harvesting was mechanized. Aircraft did all the fertilizing and spraying for pest control. By contrast, in Vietnam, the rice paddies were full of people constantly tending the crops. And women were engaged in every aspect of rice culture. They were who was growing the crop that was the basis of Vietnam's life and economy.

After a while I noticed that the women who were working out in the fields were being exposed to all the pesticides and chemicals used there. And most of those women were of childbearing age. As an environmental lawyer with an agricultural background, I was well-informed about the risks of such exposure. So I went to our friend, the renowned rice expert and agronomist, Dr. Võ-Tòng Xuân, and asked him about my concerns.

He said that the government bought these chemicals in bulk, and the containers they used in the field were not labeled. Also, that there was no training in how to use them safely. I said, "Well, how do they know how much to use?" He said they'd just done a survey on that issue and found out that everyone just used as much as they could. They also found that after using them in the fields, the women took the chemicals home and used them in their own gardens. That meant that they were doubly exposed, and that the food they ate (and the food we ate) was undoubtedly laced with some serious toxins.

The solution was suddenly obvious. I'd start an organic farm and use it as a demonstration "home garden" to show the local village women how to farm and grow their own vegetable gardens without chemicals. I'd grown organically in California and thought I could figure out how to do so in the tropics. As another benefit, this project would be an opportunity to provide information on the dangers of chemical pollution and runoff as it impacted the waterways. All the nearby factories were spewing chemical waste directly into the river, and it was not considered a problem. Maybe my farm could also provide an alternative source of income for women while addressing the growing issue of chemical pollution in the Mekong Delta.

I hired a water buffalo, and the farmer who came with it, to plow some land next to the rice facility. We cleared about 2 acres (1 hectare) of land. But I was naïve about growing food organically in the tropics. The insects, which were humongous, the plants, and every other part of the enterprise was new to me. It took me a full year to figure out how to grow the plants that people liked to eat as well as how to source local manure for fertilizer, non-chemical pest controls, and even which seeds to use.

But my cohort in all this, Sang, really helped me pull it off. He was a pleasure to work with, even though everything had to be translated back and forth for each of us. For that, I had help from the women translators who worked for Richard.

Sang and Claire at Sông Hậu Organic Farm

I also recruited women from the local university, as well as Dr. Xuân, to advise me. They were curious about these techniques too. And maybe just a bit skeptical. But, once we got going, we invited them and the local women to a lunch of foods grown on the farm, gave them a tour, and explained how we did it. Eventually, I was even asked to teach organic farming for the Ministry of Agriculture.

I found that Vietnamese women were well educated in all aspects of agriculture, either from their own experience or because their education was excellent. They quickly let me know that they were very well versed in the many ways that large multinational agricultural corporations were imposing their systems on the Third World. And I agreed with them. It led to a productive collaboration and even a conference in Cần Thơ where I was a guest speaker.

Cần Thơ women's conference on agriculture at which Claire spoke

My experience in water issues in California also provided me with an opportunity to contribute. I got involved in the water issues that were affecting the entire Mekong region. The Mekong River flows through six riparian nations—beginning in

Tibet, then through China, Thailand, Laos, and Cambodia before it fans out and covers a large delta in southern Vietnam. And while the issues there were playing out on a large international scale, they were not that different from the issues in California, which was also facing the impacts of dams, pollution, redistribution of water, salination, rampant development, farms vs. fish, and constantly contested water rights.

It was a fantastic opportunity because the region was just entering a postwar development phase. The international environmental community hoped to guide the process towards sustainability and avoid the destruction caused by unplanned development. We learned that little was known about the Mekong and its biological and cultural riches. No one had studied it yet. But these governments were fast gearing up for dam building and practically competing to destroy one of the greatest rivers and estuaries in the world. That would end the land- and water-dependent lifestyles and ancient cultures of the millions who'd farmed and fished those waters for millennia.

The more I learned about development, environment, agriculture, trade, and the politics of Southeast Asia, the more I thought I'd write about what I saw. I decided to use rice as a lens through which all those forces could be examined. So, for two years, I published a report called *The Rice Paper*. It was well subscribed and well received internationally. I also founded an NGO called The Mekong Foundation to continue working on water issues with The World Wildlife Fund in Hanoi. We did educational films on water for television. I told friends back home that our ratings were fantastic. We had 20 million viewers! Of course, I may have forgotten to mention that there was only one state-owned television channel in the delta, so those viewers had no choice but to watch whatever was broadcast.

I kept busy because I wanted to make the most of my time there, but it had also become a necessity. Richard's work took up all his time, attention, and energy. We'd intended to have a shared adventure, and sometimes we did. We traveled all over Vietnam, Laos, Cambodia, and Thailand together. We shared many good times and plenty of rough times. When I look through the journals I kept during my time in Vietnam, I frequently noted that I was glad to be there, but it was never easy.

I'd made choices that left me isolated in the Mekong Delta without a support system. My choice to live at the rice mill meant that while I was able to live and work in direct contact with people there, it was always going to be especially difficult. I was completely dependent on Richard and his company for everything I needed, and I had not anticipated how that would play out. Richard did his best, and his company was supportive. But I was not a young wife willing to live the corporate expat lifestyle of tennis and cocktail parties. I wanted to contribute to the lives of those around me as I always have in my work and life where ever I live.

Mostly, it was hard for me to be away from friends, family, and home. I had not expected to be so lonely or homesick. And then, after a few years in Vietnam, my daughter Emily was getting married, and later, our first grandchild was born. So I was traveling home more often.

A journal entry from November 1996 sums up what I was feeling at the time. I said, "I'm ending my stay in Vietnam. It's been 2 ½ years since I first came here, images of the war seared into my consciousness from the years of peace work in the 60's and 70's. I came looking for some reconciliation with that terrible war. Instead, I've been finding my own shadow."

My time in Vietnam did not end then. But that was when I crossed a line. I went from being willing to do whatever it took to make it all work, to finding an exit strategy for myself.

Looking back at that part of my experience, I must admit I was then, and still am, disappointed with myself. I really thought I was up for it. I base that assumption less on all the preparation Richard and I did or on all the efforts we made to support our stay there.

It was more about my assessment of myself at the time. I thought I had what it would take to deal with all the stress and challenges of living there. By that time, I'd studied Buddhist meditation for fifteen years, including working with the Vietnamese monk, Thích Nhất Hạnh. His peace work had begun in Vietnam during the worst of the war, and I took his teachings to heart. I tried to focus on my spiritual practice, and it was a tremendous help, when I could stay in the present moment. But far too much of the time, the loneliness and dependency and the mind-numbing heat would get me down. Some of the time it felt like I'd packed my spiritual luggage before leaving, but somehow it just never arrived once I got there.

One suggestion I was given sums up the best advice anyone could want. I asked Sulak Sivaraksa, Thai author of *Seeds of*

Peace, what I should do while I was in Vietnam. He paused a moment and said, slowly, as if speaking to a child, "Just remember to breathe in and breathe out."

I'd asked for a lot of advice, spiritual and practical, before moving to Vietnam. But I must admit that it did not occur to me to look in the funny pages. Then, on a trip home in 1996, I saw this cartoon in the paper and thought it was perfect. I still wonder what Boopsie knew that I didn't.[26]

• DOONESBURY © 1996 G. B. Trudeau. Reprinted with permission of ANDREWS MCMEEL SYNDICATION. All rights reserved.

While Vietnam is a gracious country, the daily frustrations of living there took up most of my time and energy. Everything took ten times longer than I expected, or it just didn't get done. Twenty-five years ago, there were none of the easy ways to communicate that there are now. Just sending a fax was an undertaking, and you practically had to write code to send anything electronically.

All our communications were monitored. Richard and I were constantly watched and followed. There was no privacy. So Richard and I developed a code language. And sometimes, in moments of conflict, we'd burst out laughing at the silly things we were saying. They were so idiosyncratic that we knew the translators listening in could not possibly understand what we were talking about. So, sometimes, we could turn even difficult situations into something funny.

Mostly we understood that we were there at a time of real change. When we arrived, Vietnam's postwar recovery was just getting going in earnest. The rural area where we lived was still more like the communes of the past (including twice daily propaganda broadcasts from loudspeakers on the street light posts for all to hear) than the more prosperous areas of Saigon and Hanoi. Now you can get CNN International on hotel televisions in Cần Thơ and drive all the way there from Saigon in relative comfort.

And there were moments that were exquisitely Vietnamese. At the rice facility, I was very happy to hear the morning bell that announced the start and end of the workday. It was rung near our living quarters in a rhythm that was familiar to me. It would start slowly and ring a few beats, then get faster, descending rapidly until there was a pause and then one loud resonant BONG! at the end. The reason I loved it is that it sounded so much like the bells I'd heard at the Green Gulch Farm or Tassajara Zen Buddhist retreats I loved in California. So one morning I went out early to try to find it. I waited for the ringing and followed the sound. I found it where all the workers parked their bicycles near the entrance, and I walked over to take a closer look. I did not expect a beautifully cast bronze bell like they have in Japanese temples, but I also did not expect such a beautiful sound to come out of an old iron tractor wheel being hit with a hammer either.

So that's the way it was: one moment there would be a painful difficulty, and the next was an unexpected delight. I remember long, hard, restless nights, sweating under the mosquito nets, listening to the thunder and torrential rains. I wondered what it must have been like for the young men who were fighting here, listening to the same sounds, just twenty years before. They too must have felt out of place and alone. I did. I was a middle-class white woman who was there by choice and I kept my privilege in mind. I had a beautiful garden where we'd built an aviary and filled it with tropical songbirds. I was living in what most of the women around me would consider luxury. So I was determined to learn from them about their lives and bear witness to them by hearing their stories.

One day when we were delivering rice to the orphanage in Cần Thơ, I met someone whose resilience impressed me. Vietnam, by the way, does a very good job of providing basic care for most of its people. Despite its poverty, it generally provides health care and education, and anyone who does not have family can be in an orphanage, old or young. It's an innovative way to provide care because the little ones get to live around and be cared for by the old people, and together they'd form surrogate families.

While we were there, I asked our translator to find out if anyone there would tell me their story. One woman said yes. As usual with older people, it was a story from the war. She spoke quietly. She said she was inside her home while her children and younger sister were outside playing. When she heard an airplane overhead, she ran to the door. But right then a bomb exploded in front of her. The blast killed everyone else and burned her face and arms. She was blinded. In that one moment, she lost everything. She rolled up her sleeves to show me the scars on her arms, but I could see what she might not have seen: they were also slashed across her face.

Again and again, I learned how much more complicated and horrific the war was then I'd ever imagined. And I brought those lessons home with me. Even today, 25 years later, I am continually grateful for the basics of my life: clean water, fresh air, and healthy food.

I also learned that, for most Vietnamese, the war with America had passed. They were moving on. Half the population of Vietnam had been born since the war, so they had no direct memory of it. And yet, we Americans here at home, and many of the older people in Vietnam too, still carry the wounds of that war in our minds and hearts.

Working together on this book has brought Richard and I both a renewed appreciation for all our memories of those years and all the lessons learned. But there is one more story I must tell. It will explain why I picked the word "expat" as the title of this chapter. It may seem obvious, but it's not only that.

The word is also in-joke for us because when I moved to Vietnam, my first name was Pat. By the time I left in 1998, I'd changed my name to Claire. So, literally, I am an ex-Pat. I had always wanted to change my name, and my time there presented me with the opportunity. I'd learned it was traditional to choose one's own name at mid-life in South-East Asia and that gave me permission to make the change.

There are two terms used to describe someone who goes to live in another country: "expat" and "trailing spouse." Apparently, the reason for moving determines which is best. In my case, my husband was going there for an "exciting business challenge," so he was definitely an expat. I was just joining him. That made me a trailing spouse. And looking back, it strikes me that the term is perfect and suits me better. It captures just how derivative the experience can be. When you uproot yourself; leave your home, family, and work; and move to another country to support your spouse's career, it does feel as if you are being dragged along behind the main attraction.

Finally, I am so grateful for all that Vietnam taught me. I started my career as a food and farming journalist there. My work since has been deeply informed by the vibrant local markets full of fruits, flowers, vegetables, and every kind of fish, animal, reptile, and ready-to-eat foods all being sold directly by small vendors, mostly women, of course. Would they come to welcome or eventually regret all the changes brought about by the increasing globalization and industrialization of their food system? It is not lost on me that the reason we were there was to "improve the efficiency" of rice production. Efficiency is a code word for the modernization, consolidation, and industrialization of agriculture. But for me, what's important are the lives of the small farmers and the many ways "efficiency" has destroyed them and the fundamental structures that support the way the world feeds itself.

Ironically, just as I was returning to California, a movement in the opposite direction was getting underway that was promoting sustainable agriculture, organic farming, and local food production. After I left Vietnam, I spent the next twenty years covering the tensions between industrial and sustainable agriculture.

And there is no question in my mind that the world can feed itself with healthy sufficient food for all if farmers, especially the women, are empowered in their work and the ecosystems that support sustainability are adequately supported.

My time in Vietnam was a master class in learning about the human condition as well as my own capacity. It strengthened my commitment to continue the social justice activism that began with my peace work at Cal in the 1960s. I've always understood that the work of deep moral progress may not get results in any one person's lifetime. For me though, results are not the best measure of the effort. Ultimately, I will always treasure the stories of the women that I met and the lessons learned there. Now, when I think of Vietnam, I think of their beauty and strength. I don't think of Vietnam as a war.

The problem is whether we are determined to go in the
direction of compassion or not. . . . If I lose my direction,
I have to look for the North Star, and I go to the north.
That does not mean I expect to arrive at the North Star. I
just want to go in that direction.

—Thich Nhất Hanh

Being Peace

APPENDIX 1

Wall Street Journal Reprint

THE WALL STREET JOURNAL

U.S. View

April 21, 2000

Page One Feature

In the Paddies of Vietnam, Americans Land in Quagmire

By ROBERT FRANK
Staff Reporter of THE WALL
STREET JOURNAL

Richard Mccombs

Reprinted with permission of the
Wall Street Journal

CAN THO, Vietnam—When U.S. companies parachuted back into Vietnam in 1994, the popular slogan was: "Vietnam is no longer a war. It's a market." Try telling that to corporate veterans like Richard McCombs.

Two years ago, Mr. McCombs packed up his belongings in the former Saigon, waved goodbye to his Vietnamese friends and boarded a plane back to the U.S. His multimillion-dollar effort to build a rice business in the Mekong Delta—one of the first and most prominent U.S. ventures in Vietnam—had collapsed. His local business partners had become enemies, the police were threatening to put his employees in prison, and the Communist Party attacked his company as the latest example of American imperialism.

Even now, American Rice Inc., the company Mr. McCombs worked for, and the Vietnamese government continue to fight over the liquidation of the company's in-country assets. Sitting over a bowl of Vietnamese chicken soup in his house near San Francisco recently, the soft-spoken Mr. McCombs tries to make sense of his three-year ordeal.

"I ask myself, 'Could I have done things differently?' " he says. "I'm not sure of the answer. But I do know that Vietnam is not ready to allow foreign businesses to be successful."

Twenty-five years ago this month, the last American soldiers and diplomats beat a chaotic retreat from Vietnam. Now, a second American withdrawal is on. After hundreds of American businesspeople piled into Vietnam in the mid-1990s, spending more than $1 billion on everything from auto factories and cola bottlers to power plants and steak houses, many are calling it quits amid heavy losses. U.S. investment has dropped more than 80% since 1996, to $127 million last year. U.S. companies that haven't closed altogether are cutting back their business and pulling out expatriate staff.

The problems that did in American Rice are the same ones threatening many U.S. companies in Vietnam today—poor legal protection, hostile joint-venture partners, heavy bureaucracy and a deep-seated suspicion of capitalism and foreign interests. Despite incremental legal reforms in Vietnam, Moody's Investor Service last month pointed to the country's "hesitance to allow further foreign participation in the economy" as a threat to progress.

Some of the corporate casualties: Chrysler Corp., now part of DaimlerChrysler, shelved plans for a $189 million automobile assembly plant after the Vietnam government decided to allow 14 auto makers to set up shop in the country, instead of the original three. Ford Motor Co. built a $102 million joint-venture factory with the capacity to make 14,000 cars a year. Last year it sold 400. Procter & Gamble Co. has racked up more than $30 million in losses since it set up shop, and PepsiCo is bleeding cash.

The once-lively community of American expatriates has also dried up. Keith Nolan, a guitar player who once belted out funk tunes in the bars of Ho Chi Minh City (formerly Saigon), got tired of singing to empty chairs and recently moved to Bangkok. "Most of our gigs were going-away parties," he sighs.

Investors from plenty of other countries, such as Taiwan, Korea, and Japan, are also hurting in Vietnam. Companies bear part of the blame; yes, Vietnam has 77 million people, but does it make sense to try to sell $20,000 cars to people with an average income of $300 a year?

There are some success stories like Citigroup's Citibank unit, Caterpillar Inc.'s heavy-equipment business and apparel companies such as Nike Inc.

Yet for the U.S., with its anguished history in Vietnam, the large number of corporate losses is especially painful. American Rice tells the story.

Of all the U.S. companies that flocked to Vietnam in 1994, few seemed to hold as much promise. The Houston-based rice company—the largest in the U.S.—planned to team up with a local partner to sell Vietnamese rice overseas. With American Rice hungry for supply, and Vietnam desperate for customers, the venture seemed ideal for both sides and for millions of struggling Vietnamese farmers.

On a steamy spring morning in 1994, Mr. McCombs, then American Rice's 53-year-old chief financial officer, and his wife, Claire, touched down at Ho Chi Minh City to begin their new life in the East. He was greeted by his new business partner, the elegant and powerful Duong Thi Ngoc Trieu, known as Madame Trieu.

"She was very nice ... at first," says Mr. McCombs.

To crack the Vietnamese rice market, American Rice needed a strong local ally. Rice isn't just a business in Vietnam; it is a political tool, food staple and kernel of Vietnamese culture. Employing more than 75% of Vietnamese workers, the rice business relies on extensive government subsidies and export permits to survive.

Madame Trieu seemed a promising partner for such a delicate business. As head of the largest government-owned rice exporter, Vinafood II, her empire stretched from the emerald-green paddies of the south to the marble halls of the Hanoi government. As the daughter of a former government minister and war hero, she also maintained strong ties to then-Prime Minister Vo Van Kiet.

But what started as a partnership quickly became a contest. On a hot day in mid-1994, Mr. McCombs sat on a wooden chair in Madame Trieu's meeting room for more than eight hours as she slowly chipped away at the terms of the original business plan. She refused to grant the company permits for exports, saying they would receive such quotas "as you need them." She charged American Rice new fees that more than doubled the costs of the joint venture and required American Rice to provide the $14 million in financing.

Madame Trieu, who declined to comment directly for this story but authorized several staffers and translators to speak for her, says the contract clauses were all part of the original agreement, and were "fair to both sides." Vinafood adds that export quotas can never be guaranteed to any company, since they vary according to economic circumstances.

After months of negotiating, the two companies reached agreement, and the joint venture—55%-owned by American Rice and 45%-owned by Vinafood—opened for business in late 1994. Mr. McCombs moved to Tra Noc, in the heart of Vietnam's "rice bowl," and settled into an old U.S. Army food warehouse near the rice mill.

He usually awoke at dawn and spent 12 to 13 hours a day at the mill, turning what was once a government-run supplier into an entrepreneurial start-up. He installed $1.5 million worth of high-tech equipment, raised management salaries to help stem graft and required the accountants to keep detailed records.

With no other Americans nearby, he adapted to simple village life. At sunset, he and his wife often motored down the

Mekong in a small wooden boat, gazing at the bamboo huts, longboats and families bathing their children in the river. An avid naturalist, he also built an aviary for his new collection of tropical songbirds.

No Worries

Yet a few months into the new venture, Mr. McCombs got an unwelcome surprise. A global shortage of rice caused a huge demand for Vietnamese exports, but American Rice received permits to sell only 30,000 tons of rice, well below the 120,000 planned. Unable to meet its costs, American Rice demanded an explanation from Madame Trieu.

"Don't worry, this was an unusual year," she responded, according to Mr. McCombs. "You'll get more next year." Representatives for Madame Trieu and Vinafood say American Rice was given as much quota as possible under the circumstances.

With their first season a washout, Mr. McCombs and his colleagues took a bold gamble. Turning to one of its biggest former customers, the government of Iran, American Rice won a contract to sell the country $100 million of rice, fetching the highest-ever price for Vietnamese rice. Since the Vietnam joint venture was considered a foreign entity, it was exempt from U.S. sanctions on Tehran.

American Rice was ecstatic. Madame Trieu was livid. On the eve of Tet, Vietnam's New Year, Madame Trieu, Mr. McCombs and his boss, Gerry Murphy, called a meeting to discuss the deal. Madame Trieu insisted that the contract was hers—that is to say, the government's—since "such contracts were always negotiated between governments." American Rice said the deal was theirs, won by costly marketing. Mr. Murphy said to Madame Trieu: "If you don't want to be our partner, then fine, we'll go it alone." Madame Trieu stormed out of the meeting and slammed the door. Mr. McCombs turned to Mr. Murphy and said, "I think we just won the battle and lost the war."

American Rice received about half of the Iran contract; the rest went to Vinafood and other exporters. Making matters worse, Mr. McCombs was forced to farm out much of the work to competing government exporters and to buy rice from Thailand, since it couldn't get enough export permits from Vietnam.

Mr. McCombs' radical rice-buying program stirred further controversy. Rather than buying from pricey state-owned brokers or traders, Mr. McCombs decided to purchase straight from the growers, thereby cutting costs and delivering higher prices to the farmers. He set up buying stations in remote villages and launched a "frequent seller" promotion where farmers could win radios and TVs if they came with large amounts of quality rice.

When word of the plan reached the fields, farmers poured in from around the countryside. Mr. McCombs woke up one morning to find hundreds of small wooden boats, piled with rice, tied up at the docks of the mill. An aide to Mr. McCombs whispered that some of the state-linked traders were infuriated. "He said, 'You know, it would be better politically to buy from this middleman,' " recalls Mr. McCombs.

Smiles on the Farm

Yet many rice farmers were delighted. Nguyen Van Von, a 49-year-old rice grower in the small village of Phuoc Thoi, loaded up a truck and waited outside the American Rice mill for 12 hours to make a sale. He got his highest price ever.

"The Americans were good for the rice business," says Mr. Nguyen, sitting under a mango tree on a recent morning with his wife and daughters. The government was less pleased. Said one official to American Rice: "We gave you a license to sell rice, not start a social revolution."

With poor sales, however, the joint venture's losses soared to $2 million and Vinafood officials began attacking American Rice's spending—even though Mr. McCombs' salary was $14,500 a year. During a weekly staff meeting, a former Vietcong jungle fighter who had become a Vinafood manager stood up and yelled to Mr. McCombs, "You are not doing things the Vietnamese way. The American way has failed."

Mr. McCombs shot back: "I will not have this conversation in this meeting. This is a matter for the board of directors."

It was already too late. In October 1996, the government announced that the national Inspectorate, a widely feared ministry responsible for investigating large-scale embezzlement, was launching a probe of the American Rice venture.

Mr. McCombs was baffled. "We certainly hadn't stolen anything," he says. "The only thing we could be accused of was losing money on the business, and that was because we were denied the export permits."

Investigators questioned the entire staff and combed through stacks of company receipts. American Rice staffers were threatened with jail for approving certain expenses. One of Mr. McCombs' lieutenants was asleep one night when burglars slipped in through the roof, sprayed sleeping gas on his two dogs and stole several company files and a laptop computer. The robbers were never found.

The Inspectorate concluded that American Rice had "materially violated its investment license, the laws of Vietnam and ... caused serious damage" to Vinafood. It said many of the company's expenses—including electricity bills and phone charges—were unapproved and that American Rice owed the government $1.1 million in taxes from transactions with the rice farmers.

When the report was leaked to the local press, American Rice became a lightning rod for anti-Americanism. Former U.S. Treasury Secretary Robert Rubin, touring Vietnam in 1997, was told about the case and asked the then-prime minister: "Why are you treating American Rice like this?" according to diplomatic officials who witnessed the exchange. (Through a spokesman at Citigroup, where Mr. Rubin now works, he says he doesn't recall mentioning American Rice specifically, but did stress to Vietnamese leaders the importance of creating a good environment for foreign investors.)

After incurring more than $3 million in losses, and well past his two-year commitment, Mr. McCombs called it quits. In early

1998, he packed his things in Ho Chi Minh City and boarded a plane back to San Francisco.

Today, his rice mill in Tra Noc sits quiet, with only a few workers peddling past the empty warehouses. His old aviary is gone, and the birds have vanished. The government and American Rice are squabbling over the liquidation of some of American Rice's old assets. American Rice itself just emerged from bankruptcy court; its former parent company, Los Angeles-based Erly Industries, had sought bankruptcy-law protection due to a legal dispute unrelated to Vietnam. American Rice is under new management. Officials there have no comment on the company's Vietnam experience.

Mr. McCombs, who left the company in 1998, recently took a job at a plastics-recycling company. Sitting in his kitchen, with Vietnamese folk songs playing on the CD player, Mr. McCombs pores over photographs from his Mekong days. He grows silent when he spots a photo of his former Vietnamese deputy.

"These are the people I worry about," Mr. McCombs says. "I was able to leave, but my Vietnamese friends ... they have to live with the consequences of helping me."

APPENDIX 2

Excerpts from HBS Case Study of the American Rice Investment in Vietnam

The Harvard Business School wrote a case study of the challenges and opportunities for American Rice investing in Vietnam in 1994. Excerpts from the case study are reprinted below with the permission of the Harvard Business School.[27]

Harvard Business School   9-595-020

November 15, 1994

Research Associate Quintus Travis prepared this case under the supervision of Professor Ray A. Goldberg as the basis for class discussion rather than to illustrate either effective or ineffective handling of an administrative situation.

Copyright © 1994 by the President and Fellows of Harvard College. To order copies or request permission to reproduce materials, call 1-800-545-7685 or write Harvard Business School Publishing, Boston, MA 02163. No part of this publication may be reproduced, stored in a retrieval system, used in a spreadsheet, or transmitted in any form or by any means—electronic, mechanical, photocopying, recording, or otherwise—without the permission of Harvard Business School.

American Rice, Inc. in Vietnam

From his eighteenth-floor office located in the fashionable Westwood area of Los Angeles, Gerald Murphy, Gerry to his friends, gazed over the veteran's cemetery towards Beverly Hills, deep in thought. President Clinton had removed the U.S. trade embargo on Vietnam on February 4, 1994. Within 24 hours, Gerry had flown with his son Douglas to Ho Chi Minh City and discussed the details of a planned joint venture between American Rice, Inc. and Vinafood II, Vietnam's largest rice exporter. Now, four months later, Gerry Murphy reflected on the joint venture and wondered whether it would fulfill its early promise.

The agreement that American Rice and Vinafood had signed seemed subject to a process involving constant revisions to accommodate changes and clarifications in Vietnamese law. As president and chairman of ERLY Industries, American Rice's parent company, Gerry wondered just what the final deal would look like. He was keen to identify and contain any risks associated with the project. How would the benefits derived from the venture be apportioned? How would the rice business in Vietnam develop over the longer term, and what would its effects be on ERLY Industries' other rice operations?

Doi Moi aimed to change the economic structure of the agricultural sector. Early reforms restored the household farm as the basic production unit and removed restrictions in private sector activities. The reforms also made companies more autonomous by increasing responsibility for profits and losses.

A foreigner faced three options when trying to establish business interests in Vietnam: sign a business cooperation contract, form a joint venture company, or invest in a totally foreign-owned company.

Joint venture arrangements were similar to standard international practices, but with certain distinctions. The minimum foreign contribution in a joint venture was set at 30%. Amendments, passed at the end of 1992, set the maximum duration of joint ventures at 20 years, with some exceptions allowed. Although contributions to joint ventures could be in cash or kind, the Vietnamese government was concerned about sub-standard technology being imported. The law on technical transfers was substantially tightened in 1993, to prevent foreign investors from "double dipping" their Vietnamese partners. Double dipping involved including technology as part of a capital contribution to a joint venture, and then demanding additional payment from the local partner for use of the same technology.

Despite the uncertainties related to Vietnam's business environment, foreign investment into the country was well underway by the time the U.S. embargo was removed in mid-1994, although only 7% of foreign investment was destined for the agricultural sector (Exhibit 9).Contrary to some people's expectations, the lifting of the U.S. embargo did not appear to have stimulated a rush by multinational companies into Vietnam. In a survey of multinationals conducted by the *Economist Intelligence Unit* in 1994, concerns were expressed over the smoothness of implementation of Vietnam's economic reforms. Political instability and inadequacies in the legal system were perceived to be two particular risks associated with establishing business in Vietnam. According to one firm, the greatest risk was "lack of certainty that the government can/will deliver projects without second guessing by other government sectors."

ARI's interest in Vietnam mirrored the relaxation of U.S. trade policy towards the country. On December 14, 1992, the U.S. government took a major step towards lifting the self-imposed embargo against Vietnam by authorizing U.S. companies to open offices, conduct feasibility studies, and sign contracts in the country.

In response to the relaxation of American policy, American Rice decided to investigate the Vietnamese rice market. ARI realized that it was inseparably linked to the global rice industry. Although U.S. rice consumption and export tonnage were rising, the U.S. share of world rice trading was in decline and U.S. rice imports were rising. An ARI review of rice source diversity, which studied six countries, identified Vietnam as a market that offered consistent, exportable, rice volumes. Furthermore, Vietnam's traditional export markets did not significantly overlap those of ARI or other U.S. exporters. Vietnam also offered low cost rice production, room for expansion, and appeared to be increasingly business friendly.

Outstanding Issues

A second set of issues related to the appointment of a General Director for the venture. Gerry Murphy wondered what skills the position would require and where he could find a suitable candidate for the post. Richard McCombs, Chief Financial Officer at ERLY Industries, and Executive Vice

President of Finance at ARI, had volunteered for the position. Richard held a Stanford MBA, had experience in consulting, and had been President of a wine company purchased by ERLY in 1987. Nonetheless, Murphy wondered how this related to the demands of management in Vietnam, and American Rice-Vinafood in particular. If Richard was appointed General Director, the question of how ERLY Industries would be affected by the departure of its CFO remained on Murphy's mind. Assuming Richard was appointed, Murphy further considered what advice he should offer Richard about where to start focusing his efforts as the new General Director of American Rice-Vinafood.

Other issues Murphy faced were more abstract, but nonetheless important. Gerry Murphy perceived apparent contradictions in the Vietnamese business environment and rice industry. Notably, Vinafood II lacked experience of operating in a market system. Murphy reflected on how this would affect the joint venture relationship. Which aspects of the agreement should ARI remain flexible on? Was it ARI's responsibility to educate its Vietnamese partner as to the ways of the market? Murphy was aware of his fiduciary duty to maximize shareholder value, but what did this mean in the present circumstances?

Acknowledgments

1) *Moby Dick* by Herman Melville for the inspiration to write this book

2) Claire Cummings, who edited this book diligently

3) Now Society cartoon by William Hamilton reprinted from 9/4/1994 issue of *Newsweek* with permission of YGS Group

4) *Wall Street Journal* April 21, 2000, by Robert Frank reprinted with permission of Copyright Clearance Center

5) Harvard Business School case study titled *American Rice, Inc. in Vietnam* reprinted with permission of Harvard Business Publishing

6) Doonesbury cartoon by Garry Trudeau reprinted with permission of Andrews McMeel Syndication

Notes

1   Ray A Goldberg and Quintus Travis, *American Rice, Inc. in Vietnam* (Harvard Business School, Case 595-020, November 1994).

2   Tina Grant, *International Directory of Company Histories*, Vol. 33. (Detroit: St. James Press, 2000).

3   Murray Hiebert, *Vietnam Notebook* (Clarenton, VT: Tuttle Publishing, 1995).

4   G.L. Denning and Võ-Tòng Xuân, eds., *Vietnam and IRRI: A Partnership in Rice Research, Proceedings of a Conference Held in Hanoi, Vietnam, 4-7 May 1994* (International Rice Research Institute, 1995).

5   USDA, *Rice Situation Report,* October 1994.

6   Huu Ngoc, ed., *Vietnamese Folk-Tales: Satire and Humour* (Hanoi, Vietnam: The Gioi Publishers, 2002).

7   Thomas R. Hargrove, *A Dragon Lives Forever: War and Rice in Vietnam's Mekong Delta 1969-1991, and Beyond* (New York: Ballantine Books, 1994).

8   Keynote speech by Minister of Agriculture Nguyễn Công Tạn. See note 4 above.

9   See note 4 above.

10   History of Vietnam-IRRI cooperation paper presented by Võ-Tòng Xuân. See note 4 above.

11   See note 4 above.

12   See note 4 above.

13   Andreas Augustin, *Sofitel Metropole Hanoi (The Most Famous Hotels in the World)* (Friends of the Most Famous Hotels in the World, 2008).

14   See note 3 above.

15   Viet Nam Fine Arts Museum Guide (Hanoi, Vietnam: The Gioi Publishers).

16   Geoffrey Clifford and John Balaban, *Vietnam: The Land We Never Knew* (San Francisco: Chronicle Books Llc, 1989).

17   Huu Ngoc and Lady Borton, eds., Pho: A Specialty of Hanoi (Vietnamese Culture: Frequently Asked Questions) (Hanoi, Vietnam: The Gioi Publishers, 2008).

18   Kendra Pierre-Louis, "We finally know how durian got so stinky: It's one funky fruit," Popular Science, October 9, 2017, https://www.popsci.com/why-durian-smells-bad/.

19   Lucas Reilly, "20 Attempts to Describe the Taste of Durian, the World's Smelliest Fruit," Mental Floss, December 7, 2018, https://www.mentalfloss.com/article/565968/attempts-describe-taste-durian-worlds-smelliest-fruit.

20   George J. Church, "Saigon," Time magazine, June 24, 2001, http://content.time.com/time/magazine/article/0,9171,134054,00.html.

21   Pete Peterson's comment at U.S. Embassy in Hanoi 1997.

22   CNN broadcast May 9, 1997.

23   Robert Frank, "In the Paddies of Vietnam, Americans Land in Quagmire," Wall Street Journal, updated April 21, 2000, https://www.wsj.com/articles/SB956273388525695150.

24   See previous note.

25   Pete Peterson: Assignment Hanoi, PBS, 1999, Sandy Northrop Producer.

26   Doonesbury cartoon by Garry Trudeau.

27   See note 1 above.